HONG KONG
IN THE MOUTH OF THE DRAGON

香港

Pierre Cayrol

Charles E. Tuttle Company
Rutland, Vermont & Tokyo, Japan

To Paul and Julie

Published by Charles E. Tuttle Publishing,
an imprint of Periplus Editions (HK) Ltd.

LCC Card No. 98-87068
ISBN 0-8048-2115-1

First edition, 1998

Originally published in 1997 as *Hong Kong: Dans la guele du dragon*
by Editions Philippe Picquier Collection Reportages

Printed in Singapore

Distributed by:

USA **Charles E. Tuttle Co., Inc.**
Airport Industrial Park
RR1 Box 231-5
North Clarendon, VT 05759
Tel: (802) 773-8930
Fax: (802) 773-6993

Japan **Tuttle Shokai, Inc.**
1-21-13 Seki
Tama-ku, Kawasaki-shi
Kanagawa-ken 214, Japan
Tel: (81) (44) 833-0225
Fax: (81) (44) 822-0413

Southeast Asia
Berkeley Books Pte Ltd.
5 Little Road #08-01
Singapore 536983
Tel: (65) 280-3320
Fax: (65) 280-6290

Tokyo Editorial Office:
2-6, Suido 1-chome,
Bunkyo-ku, Tokyo 112, Japan

Boston Editorial Office:
153 Milk Street, 5th Floor
Boston, MA 02109, USA

Singapore Editorial Office:
5 Little Road #08-01
Singapore 536983

Contents

Introduction

History in Reverse

Hong Kong, the Mecca of capitalism—in the grips of a Communist bureaucracy. Not long ago such an image would have provoked derisive laughs, as likely as Belgium falling under Congolese jurisdiction or Britain becoming a territory of Grenada.

And yet this time, fantasy has become reality. The dictatorial and archaic Chinese system is going to penetrate (or get lost in?) the temple of high-tech liberalism. It is history in reverse.

At the stroke of midnight on June 30, 1997, under a pelting rain . . . the red star-studded flag of the People's Republic of China replaced the Union Jack on every mast in all of Hong Kong's public spaces.

Abruptly, Prince Charles and Hong Kong's last colonial governor, Chris Patten, both soaked to the skin by the storm, gave the torch to the man who is so cherished in Beijing: Tung Chee-hwa, the first Chief Executive of the brand new Special Administrative Region.

A Smooth Transition—One Year Later

At this time, one would have expected a radical mutation, an authentic revolution in daily life. But this has not occurred. Even the most ardent anti-communist has to admit that, at a glance, nothing has changed. Nothing!

The Communist regime, usually so clumsy and brutal, showed itself in a new aspect, noticeably wiser and more diplomatic than was feared when Hong Kong returned to Chinese rule. Is this the mark of China's newest rising star, Prime Minister Zhu Rongji? Perhaps. But one thing is certain—on the surface, at least, daily life has not changed dramatically.

It was all so organized, even mundane: Chinese soldiers replaced British sailors in the barracks at Fort Stanley, vacated by the Royal Navy. The soldiers of the People's Liberation Army are notably discreet. They are nowhere to be seen outside their barracks. On orders from their commanders, they do not mix with the local population. The harbor brothels feel deserted. The seats at Suzie Wong's bars in Wanchai are empty. Prostitutes from Manila and Bangkok are sorely disappointed. The glorious PLA never stands down; it stays out of sight, in the shadows.

In the heart of Hong Kong there is a military barracks that is richly symbolic. The barracks has kept its old colonial name—the Prince of Wales.

After 155 years of colonization, Hong Kong, symbol of commerce and haven for liberty, has fallen under an impoverished and tyrannical system. The scruffy, authoritarian uncle has shown up on his gilded nephew's doorstep. This epochal moment went almost unremarked.

No one expected "Hong Kong 1997" to be another "Shanghai 1949" or "Tiananmen 1989." The People's Army did not march on Hong Kong, exacting tributes or crushing students with its tanks. Missionaries were not run out of town, prostitutes were not sent into exile, nor were banks nationalized. But who would have expected such a peaceful and quiet handover?

Symbols have remained unchanged, with a few exceptions. The profile of Queen Elizabeth has been removed from all coins and stamps. The prestigious Royal Jockey Club has erased all references to the Crown. That is all!

Street names have not changed. Queen's Street is still there, the main artery in the heart of the city. Policemen have not exchanged their uniforms for those worn by mainland police. On the surface, the sleight of hand performed by London and Beijing proceeded without any blood or tears.

But we should not be satisfied with appearances.

Defending "Chinese Values"

After the handover, so far liberties have not been trampled. Street demonstrations still occur, even those directed at the leadership in Beijing. In the course of one year, the police have used physical force only once. In September 1997, during the annual meeting of the International Monetary Fund, Li Peng, then China's Prime Minister and now President of the National People's Congress, visited Hong Kong. Police clubbed a handful of people who were demonstrating peacefully against the presence of the "Butcher of Tiananmen." Since this incident, no other police violence has been reported.

The courageous Emily Lau, a former BBC reporter elected as a lawmaker under the British rule, but stripped of her office when the Chinese came with a new Parliament in tow, has multiplied her initiatives. Access to the local mainstream media has become somewhat more difficult for her. But she can still express herself without fear. She condemns what she describes as the slow but steady seizure of local control by the new regime.

The owners of Hong Kong's newspapers swear oaths that their editorial freedom has not been infringed at all since the handover. At the *South China Morning Post,* the territory's main English-language newspaper, management proclaims that the arrival of the Chinese has not changed its policies. This creed must be qualified somewhat, however. In private, many local journalists confess that their pens have become suddenly heavier, that self-censorship is setting in, for fear of incurring the Chinese censors' wrath.

Yet, it must be said that despite the constant watch of human rights

NGOs, not one case of outright censorship has been reported so far. Hong Kong journalists have simply become more cautious.

In the spring of 1998, Xu Siming, an octogenarian official in Beijing, blasted RTHK,the public radio and television network in Hong Kong, for being "anti-Chinese." Chief Executive Tung Chee-hwa and his deputy, Anson Chan, both proclaimed that freedom of the press should be protected in Hong Kong. They could hardly say anything else, considering the uneasiness Xu created in the Hong Kong press.

At first glance, the daily life and commerce remained unchanged. This may very well be the case. But with the passing months, the new regime has begun systematically defending "Chinese values" against the "colonialist culture." And this is revealing.

Colonized First by the British, Now by the Chinese

These days, show business celebrities appear on television dressed in People's Liberation Army uniforms!

Tung Chee-hwa misses no opportunity to praise the "values" imported from the mainland, which are supposed to give Hong Kong a new face and restore its pride, which had been trampled on by the British. The new boss in Hong Kong—and he admits it privately—wishes to depoliticize the island. He wants to instill a nationalist pride in the people of Hong Kong, unite an anomalous population, and remove from them any idea of challenging the newly established order.

Tung's model is obviously Singapore. Lee Kuan-Yew, father of Singapore's democracy, believes that collective weal takes precedence over individual freedoms. As author Ian Buruma points out, like the Singapore strong man, Tung distrusts the parliamentarian system as one prone to create "subversive and divisive" practices.

In this regard, Mr. Tung may be sanguine. He did not have to do much to silence the parliament. He simply had to follow London's lead, adopting only a slightly more authoritarian note. As was the case under British rule,in the first democratic elections under the Chinese regime in May

1998, only one-third of the sixty-member legislature was elected. The rest of the members were picked by local organized institutions. Thirty were selected by different sectors of the economy, or functional constituencies, and ten by an election committee composed primarily of officials sympathetic to Beijing.

The only overtly anti-parliament change instituted by the new re-gime has been a revision of the electoral law which, in effect, diminished the chamber's popular representation. The British had inaugurated a majority ballot system which allowed the Democratic Party, the main opposition party led by Martin Lee, to win the last election of the colonial era. Tung Chee-hwa's friends, advised by the leaders in Beijing, have for their part established a proportional ballot system which has given rise to a myriad of small parties, most of them supportive of the Communist regime.

Gradually, politics, which had been of little importance in Hong Kong before the handover, is becoming even less attractive to the populace. It is often said that Hong Kong's people care only about business and cannot be bothered with politics. This is only partly true. After all, if the people of Hong Kong are apolitical, it is mainly because the British barred them from truly participating in the territory's governance. Chris Patten may say whatever he pleases, but the fact remains that only the Chinese who were close to London were considered "good" and rewarded as such.

On the whole, Hong Kong's people did not notice a great political change after the handover. Previously colonized by the British, they are now colonized by the Chinese.

The Law of Wheeling and Dealing

On the surface, nothing seems to have changed in Hong Kong's courts. They are under no direct pressure from the Communist regime. Judges, most of whom were appointed by the British, insist that they are completely independent. What is more, the Independent Commission Against Corruption (ICAC), established by the British, continues to investigate at full tilt, as it had been prior to the handover. In April 1998, the ICAC ordered the arrest of customs officials who had been involved in the trade of pirated compact disks with the mainland.

In the realm of jurisprudence, nothing has changed—but how long will that last?

Before the handover, businessmen, even Chinese businessmen, would settle in Hong Kong to take advantage of its exemplary modern legal system. The territory had a comprehensive commercial code ruling businesses.

In the ex-British colony, a written contract could not be breached. *Dura lex, sed lex*. The law was obeyed. Decidedly British-looking magistrates in curly white wigs punished transgressors without mercy. Today,the wigs have disappeared. But the law continues to be observed in Hong Kong.

Yet, abuses are still to be feared. Many analysts worry about Chinese law gradually taking root in Hong Kong. The Chinese legal code is outdated, contradictory, and incomplete even when it is respected. Chinese statutes have only one aim—to strengthen the State's power.

At the People's Palace in Beijing, one year after the handover, officials are still celebrating. What sweet revenge it was on those colonialists who plundered the rock at the end of the scandalous Opium War in 1841. Yet, during the opening of negotiations with the British in September 1982, the Chinese were not at all prepared to have the island's statutes modified. They quickly understood that by reforming Hong Kong, they would lose in a flash all the benefits this capitalist platform at their doorstep had to offer as a transit point for their goods to the West, which has provided hundreds of businesses located in the south a chance to operate in a healthy legal environment.

The historical paradox is that it was the English who pressured the Chinese. Margaret Thatcher, afraid of a steady influx of Asian boat people via Hong Kong, preferred to dispose of the rocky appendage which was a potential long-term danger. She accomplished this through a clever stratagem.

As Robert Cottrell recounts in his book *The End of Hong Kong,* Thatcher saw that it was impossible to get the Chinese to negotiate without certain preliminaries, and she tried to establish a decree stipulating that London would hand over "sovereignty" of Hong Kong to Beijing, but would retain territorial "administration." A furious Deng Xiaoping categorically rejected this proposal, affirming that the two made up an "indivisible whole."

After extensive negotiations Thatcher, advised by Britain's ambassador to Beijing, Sir Percy Cradock, modified her position until at last she gave in altogether. Many accounts by contemporary historians point out that Thatcher agreed to Deng's terms to forestall a tidal wave of immigration from Hong Kong into Great Britain, which she feared she would have been unable to control.

London Seals the Fate of Six Million Subjects

Unconcerned with its moral obligations, London chose decolonization over integration with one stroke of the pen, handing over the fate of six million people to the People's Republic of China on a silver platter, without ever seeking their opinion on the matter.

A wonderful example of England's concern for its Hong Kong subjects is the piecemeal manner in which only a scant few British passports were issued. Worse, in order to prevent immigration, Great Britain invented special documents reserved for non-English citizens, the "British National Overseas" passports (BNO) or the "British Dependent Territories Citizen" passports (BDTC), custom-made for overseas use. In the terms of the Hong Kong British Nationality Order 1986, these passports granted the right to travel to, but prohibited the right to reside or work in Great Britain. An ingenious form of discrimination, which created *de jure* two types of British subjects: the nationals or "good English," and the rest, those in Hong Kong mainly, a subcategory forbidden to settle in the same United Kingdom which had colonized them for more than a century.

The decision to institute the BNOs led to a major yearly exodus of roughly 60,000 of Hong Kong's wealthiest citizens per year to Canada and Australia; this continued throughout the 1990s. The majority of these emigrés returned shortly before Hong Kong's reunification with China after obtaining abroad what Great Britain had refused them—foreign nationality. These proud new Australian or Canadian subjects can now pack up and leave Hong Kong in event of an emergency.

Only certain minorities—7,500 Indians and Pakistanis, in particular—were finally able to obtain English citizenship after a difficult struggle. This should allow them to remain peacefully in Hong Kong. If London had not shown such "generosity" through an agreement made in *extremus* in January 1997, they would have been "stateless" individuals, since the Chinese refused to integrate them into the Special Administrative Region.

How could London have hesitated for so long, considering that so many of these Indians had tremendously contributed to Hong Kong's success? The Star Ferry shuttle linking Hong Kong to Kowloon was the work of an Indian, Dorabji Naorojee. One of the first presidents of the Hong Kong and Shanghai Banking Corporation at the end of the 1800s was also an Indian by the name of Belilios. Not to mention the anti-tuberculosis center opened ages ago by another Indian, Dhun Ruttonjee. The work of these Indians should have made their compatriots worthy of a passport without a moment's hesitation.

Even the Gurkhas, the valiant Nepalese soldiers of the Royal Army, who fought fearlessly to defend the flag of the British Empire, had to keep stamping their feet until the very last moment, January 1997, when their families were finally allowed to accompany them to England.

The Iron Lady Presses the Chinese

The negotiations between China and Great Britain lasted two years, the time limit set by China. Within that time, the two sides agreed that Hong

Kong would revert to Chinese rule on July 1, 1997, thanks to the skillfulness of the "Iron Lady" who quickly turned into a "Velvet Lady."

Today, the Communist Chinese authorities have landed a fortune for their kindhearted attitude. They claim they are happy to recover Hong Kong, certain they will continue to benefit from Hong Kong's role as a trade "stopover" and place of finance. The slogan "one country, two systems," coined by Deng Xiaoping, gives them hope and an outlet.

With calculators in their hands, they are delighting in the handover, adding up the huge profits piling up in this skyscraper-studded land, the vital point of contact between Asia and the rest of the world. To understand this better, we have to go back one and a half centuries.

Born of the Rape of China

Henry Tran Van Kha brilliantly characterized Hong Kong as "a juvenile delinquent, whose birth resulted from the rape of a decadent, corrupt and venal China by a drug-trafficking, Mob-infested England."

As early as 1830, the English opium dealers, genuine British lords, were the first sniffing out the gold they could rake in from Hong Kong. In the middle of the eighteenth century, after closing the Chinese ports to international trade, English traders were having an increasingly hard time making money. Business slowed to a crawl. Only Canton, in southern China, was open to traders during the winter months to stock up on silk and teas, items highly prized in England.

But Chinese merchants were becoming greedy, demanding increasing amounts of silver, furs, and textiles in exchange. With opium bought in Bengal, the English found the perfect solution—drugs in exchange for silk and tea. Royal Navy frigates shamelessly escorted cargo and protected the drug trade.

In 1839, after a few prosperous years, things fell apart. Manchurian China, worried that its silver reserves were dwindling to dangerously low levels, sent the imperial administrator Lin Tse-hsu to Canton demanding the English to surrender their drugs, their "foreign filth." The non-

Chinese quarter was closed off. After a forty-day siege, twenty thousand trunks containing fifteen hundred tons of opium were handed over to the authorities. The English merchants, ordered to leave by Captain Charles Elliot, representative of the Crown in Canton, withdrew to Macao, swearing they would come back.

One year later, in February 1840, the Foreign Office Secretary, Lord Palmerston, was persuaded by two of the richest opium traders, the Scotsmen William Jardine and James Matheson (their multibillion dollar company still bears their names in Hong Kong), to dispatch a British naval expedition. The four thousand-man expeditionary force was stationed in India, ready to spring into action.

In the British Parliament, a few voices of opposition protested. William Gladstone even spoke in support of the "justified right" of the Chinese to fight against a "scandalous and atrocious policy" based on the drug trade. His words went unheeded.

The Opium Wars

The first Opium War broke out in June 1840. After a few cannon shots, the English occupied the Zhou Shan islands at the mouth of the Yangtze River. The Chinese were forced to negotiate.

Captain Elliot's goal was to gain sovereignty over Hong Kong (Chinese for "Perfumed Port"), separated from the mainland by the mile-wide Kowloon Strait, and set up a commercial base. The island was situated less than a hundred miles from Canton and had a deep harbor. A calm secluded creek endowed with plenty of advantages allowed the British Empire and its traders to carry on their drug traffic.

Elliot succeeded. In the Chaunbi Convention of January 26, 1841, the Chinese promised to relinquish Hong Kong. A British ship hoisted the Union Jack over the "rock." But the English were not satisfied. Lord Palmerston, head of the diplomatic corps, felt that Elliot could have gotten more: first and foremost, an outlet for Western trade to the entire

Chinese continent. Elliot was removed and sent away as a trade official in the new Republic of Texas.

The agreement was soon disavowed by both countries. Hostilities mounted following a disagreement over the right of the Chinese to search British boats anchored at Chinese ports. The incident was set up by the English, who were seeking a pretext for a confrontation.

The English army, commanded by Lord Elgin, won again. The 1842 Nanking Treaty forced China to hand Hong Kong over to England, open up five ports to foreigners (Canton, Shanghai, Ningbo, Amoy, Fuzhou), and pay damages for losses incurred by opium traders.

On January 26, 1843, Hong Kong officially became a British colony. Its first Governor, Sir Henry Pottinger, predicted that "the island would quickly become a vast center of trade and affluence."

Obviously he was right. The economy prospered at lightning speed. In March 1860, after the Second Opium War, the Beijing Convention gave the British a mainland Chinese beachhead on the Kowloon Peninsula; they also obtained a permanent lease as a means "to maintain law and order in the Hong Kong port and its surroundings." The English knew this peninsula well; it is where they used to play cricket.

As a final move, following Great Britain's demand to extend its "borders" for security reasons, the Chinese agreed to lease them the New Territories and two hundred thirty-six islands on June 9, 1898 for a period of ninety-nine years.

History has come full circle. The lease expired.

Today England has no more opium to sell. It has given back to Caesar what was his in the first place, a "rock nobody had ever heard of" which England made prosper, to quote Lord Palmerston.

One Country, Two Systems

On July 1, 1997, Hong Kong became a "Special Administrative Region"), according to the terms set forth in Article 31 of the Chinese Constitution.

For fifty years, it will retain its capitalist system. This is all stipulated in the Basic Law, a mini-Constitution, as it is called by the media, which went into effect on July 1, cementing the territory's future until the year 2047. The sixty-nine page text, which was formally adopted on April 4, 1990 by the People's Congress in Beijing, was subject to a decree signed by the Congress president, Yang Shankun.

The preamble of this document is straightforward:

> The People's Republic of China has decided . . . that Hong Kong will become a Special Administrative Region . . . that, in accordance with the principle 'One country, two systems' [a slogan coined by Deng Xiaoping], the socialist system will not be practiced in Hong Kong.

Article 5 also specifies that "the outdated capitalist system and its lifestyle will remain in place for 50 years." In case the reader still does not understand, the next article stipulates: "the Special Administrative Region of Hong Kong will protect property rights, in accordance with the law."

The laws currently in effect will not be modified, but can be amended (Article 8). Freedom of expression, assembly and the press will be guaranteed (Article 27), as well as religious freedom (Article 32).

Personal freedom will be "inviolable," and no Hong Kong resident can be arrested arbitrarily (Article 28).

Lastly, the island will enjoy a "high degree of autonomy" (Article 12). Only issues relevant to the Foreign Affairs Ministry or Defense Ministry will be handled by the "People's Central Government" (Articles 13 and 14). In other words, Beijing. Matters involving the maintenance of law and order in the region will be dealt with by the Hong Kong government (Article 14).

So much for the theory. For now, the People's Republic of China seems willing to keep its promises. Freedoms that are brutally repressed on the mainland are still respected in Hong Kong.

Of course, no one can predict the future of Hong Kong with any certainty, neither the optimists (or their pretenders), such as the business community, nor the Communists' fiercest critics who, one year after the handover, continue to envision a dire fate for the territory.

What is certain: Since the departure of the British, the Hong Kong economy has endured serious setbacks. The territory's problems are not due to the handover itself but the economic crisis gripping all of Asia.

Daily life in Hong Kong is no longer as pleasant as it once was. The champagne flows less freely in clubs, business is less robust. The stock market is depressed. Shares of mainland Chinese companies (the "red chips") are no longer so attractive. Expatriates are tired of paying exorbitant rents for their homes and are beginning to leave for other places. Vacancies are rising. The construction sector, the only tangible form of wealth in Hong Kong, is starting to show cracks. Japanese and American tourists, frightened by rising prices, head for other Asian nations whose currencies have been severely depreciated. Beach resorts in Thailand and Indonesia are bargains with the baht and rupiah losing so much ground.

Every effort has been made to keep the Hong Kong dollar pegged to the US dollar. Chinese leaders, especially Prime Minister Zhu Rongji and Hong Kong Chief Executive Tung Chee-hwa, reiterate that the "peg" will never go away. This remains to be seen. There is little room for optimism. Superlative Hong Kong has lost its winner's smile and is struggling to recover its former glory.

The Chinese Communists have done their part in Hong Kong's recovery, injecting massive amounts of money into the stock market during the recent monetary crisis. Hong Kong remains a formidable trump card for Beijing. Its foreign exchange reserves are still the world's third largest.

Yet, caution is in order. The winds may soon change. We stil see countless corruption cases as well as human-rights violations. The People's Republic of China is by no means heading toward democracy, and the recent release of high-profile dissidents, such as Wang Dan, the Tiananmen Square student hero, should not be misunderstood.

Beijing wants to open up its economy, following the road blazed by Deng Xiaoping. In the political field, however, Beijing is still adamantly maintaining the Communist Party dictatorship. This line has been reaffirmed at the Chinese Communist Party's fifteenth congress.

To conclude, one must understand that China will not hesitate to demolish the remaining advantages Hong Kong offers if they represent the slightest threat to the Communist regime. Hong Kong, the Chinese-style goose with the golden eggs, is ailing. If she were to infect her neighbors, her masters in Beijing would kill her, without hesitation.

The Shameful Face

Is Hong Kong the Chinatown of the People's Republic?
Unless some miraculous metamorphosis occurs, the Chinese Communists will gradually introduce their way of living, which involves corruption, bribes, and shady wheeling and dealing, into Hong Kong. Until now, Hong Kong was more or less spared. English law reigned. But how will things evolve now that the two systems have merged?

Many top Chinese leaders have a *sui generis* view of the economic and financial worlds. They see "little gifts" as a normal mode of operating and do not conceal the practice. A survey conducted by the university in the centrally located Chinese town of Wuhan showed that 54% of the people surveyed "pay off the authorities" to resolve important matters.

In order to settle a business deal behind the Great Wall, *guanxi* and contacts are often more important than money. One needs influential friends, people high in the Party ranks, who are there when the time comes to pull out a file and place it on the top of the pile, with a favorable mention. One has good reason to fear that these mainland habits, which have grown into actual customs, will poison Hong Kong, once the British legal system has disappeared.

At any rate, Yang Ti Liang, former head of Justice under the British administration, and a dismayed former candidate for the position of First Chief of the Executive in the post-colonial period, is worried. He has spoken and written about his concerns on several occasions.

The Case of Zhou, Deng Xiaoping's Friend

This high-ranking magistrate has taken off his wig and judge's robe, but he remains careful. Without daring to directly attack People's China, he fears for the future of the Chinese on the island. Like all of Hong Kong's public officials, he knows that the cases of corruption among businessmen with close ties to Beijing are legion.

Yang Ti Liang delights in recounting the affair that brought the downfall of Zhou Beifang, 42, the son of the former president of China's largest steel corporation, Capital Iron & Steel, and none other than a friend of the patriarch Deng Xiaoping.

From 1992 to 1995, Zhou Beifang, who was based in Hong Kong. built up an empire estimated at about $1.5 billion. His company, Shougang Concord International Enterprises, Ltd., was one of the most highly rated on the Exchange. Its share prices rose by more than 700% in 1992 and 1993. Zhou acquired a reputation as a man of power, openly discussing his family connections in public. In Hong Kong, he owned three homes and five luxury cars.

Once a symbol of grandeur and decadence, Zhou today is locked up in a Chinese prison. He was sentenced to death, which was later commuted to life imprisonment, for having accepted $1.2 million in bribes. What is more, he concocted a plan to corrupt various Chinese officials by proposing to move their families—especially the women—to Hong Kong.

Ostensibly, the case of Zhou should have reassured Hong Kong's elite that the Chinese are not entirely lax about enforcing their laws. But that was far from the case. While Zhou's conviction confirmed Beijing's apparent determination to combat corruption, it also showed how widespread and high-reaching it is. Many foreign investors in

Hong Kong, once they have gotten over their initial blind optimism about the cleverness of the slogan "one country, two systems," start to wonder whether Beijing has any intention of putting it into practice. No sooner did these business people expressed their faith in the future to any-one who would listen, especially in the French press, than they began having doubts. After the handover, they fear that they will have to reach into their pockets for the smallest transaction. It is a real risk, and not the only one.

A Private Criminal Club

The widespread corruption in China is not the only danger to Hong Kong. The mainland may just as well export a hodgepodge of sordid enterprises—embezzlement, smuggling, drugs, prostitution.

Hong Kong has been getting ready. You might even think that the island has been ready for some time. In spite of its seemingly calm, orderly and regulated way of life, the territory has known a long past of criminal violence. Until now, the well-organized English authorities' role was that of a moderating filter. Law and order was enforced with utmost efficiency.

Vice, depravity, violence of every kind, opium dens, underground gambling rooms, and arms trafficking have existed for sure, but everything has gone on discreetly behind closed doors. Hong Kong has been a big private club, reserved for the initiated. Sin was kept hidden under an impenetrable bell jar.

A Chinese Havana

The worst fear is that Hong Kong will eventually become an Asian hybrid of Panama City and Las Vegas—or even a Chinese Havana.

Hong Kong might very well overtake all the other megalopolises of sex, replacing Manila, for example, where local authorities have given the sidewalks a good cleaning. Even Bangkok, the regional capital of debauchery, risks losing some of its business.

The international police have no doubt: opening the border between Hong Kong and mainland China will provide a golden opportunity for the triads, the gangs and the Chinese mob. They will be able to join forces, organize, expand their market, and reinforce their contacts.

Crime, drugs, prostitution, and gambling will spread. Hong Kong, with its prime location, could become the new dumping ground of Southeast Asia.

There are already plenty of potbellied Western tourists who are deserting Thailand and the Philippines to venture into the People's Republic, where the brothels and massage parlors are incredibly cheap. The Special Economic Zone of Shenzhen, one hour from Hong Kong by train, and the southern island of Hainan, both on Chinese territory, are reaping in the profits. Prices have been slashed, a consequence of the misery.

Hong Kong could be next. We are starting to witness a globalization process, even in the sex business. As certain Asian countries are developing, salaries are improving, in the sex industry as well as others. Despite its economic success, Communist China is still going to have to wait a long time before it can feed its 1.2 billion inhabitants properly—and wipe out prostitution. Tourists, ever on the prowl for cheap sex, have nothing to fear; the Chinese amazons will not be raising their fees any time soon.

Hong Kong is going to be a melting pot welcoming hundreds of prostitutes from the southern part of the mainland, drawn to the port's neon lights. To adapt to the local market, prices and living standards will be lowered. Hong Kong's permissive luxury will be replaced by a Chinese clearance sale.

The Communists in Beijing are exposing themselves to what could turn out to be a shocking eye-opener. The seemingly naive apprentice may unwittingly outdo his master. Hong Kong could become China's back-alley dive. In any case, the signs are strong.

TRIADS
A State within a State

Call her Jenny. She runs a shop in Kowloon in the Tsim Sha Tsui section of the tourist district, where all the palace hotels face the sky-scraper-dotted bay. The prices here are higher than anywhere else between the Peninsula and Marriott Hotels.

Business is going well for Jenny. Yet her main enterprise is in jeopardy. This young Cantonese woman, a former drug dealer, is not a typical shopkeeper. She is an informer for the Hong Kong police, set up to manage this store with the specific goal of luring the triads.

Blackmail, Extortion, and the Interior Decorator

Seated under a wheezing ceiling fan in his Mongkok police-station office on a hot and muggy spring afternoon, Detective Chief Inspector Paul S. Renouf, a hefty man in his forties whose specialty is the anti-triad campaign, is disappointed.

"We thought we could easily catch them red handed by opening up this shop, but no one's shown up for the time being. Usually it's the same old story. Whether it happens to be a nightclub or some shop, the triads propose—or rather impose!—the services of a decorator. It is their way of extorting a tribute. If the shopkeeper accepts their offer, no problem. Once the decorator has finished the job, he raises his fee and gives a commission to his 'protectors.' Otherwise, the triads set the place on fire and no one is the wiser. No complaints are lodged, no investigations made—it's just written off as an accident!"

All of Hong Kong's shops, with the exception of the large supermarkets, are victims of extortion. The gangs have divided up the territory and each controls its own sector. Kowloon's Jordan Road which swarms with tourists crowding into the flourishing photo and jewelry shops, is watched carefully and taxed. So is Nathan Road. In order to be left in peace, the shop managers pay their "dues" and regularly have their stores redecorated. It is a longstanding custom in Hong Kong.

As soon as a shop owner applies for a license to open up a karaoke or a shoe store, a triad member drops by for a visit. They start talking about decoration, and before the owner knows it, the extortion begins.

Funeral parlors are also hounded by the triads. A crematorium located at the southern end of the island, near the surfers' paradise, Big Waves Bay, has often been the scene of armed combat between rival gangs.

Paul Renouf remembers the fire at Top One, a karaoke bar in the Tsim Sha Tsui area. In January 1997, fifteen customers were asphyxiated or burned alive. The owner had refused to pay the required "tax," so six fifteen-year-old members of the Sun Yee On gang—four boys and two girls—showered the place with Molotov cocktails.

Even on the highways, at the China-Hong Kong border, truck drivers are held up.

China's Highwaymen

In the chilly wee hours of a Tuesday in October, near the checkpoint of Lok Ma Chau at the Chinese border, the truck drivers are furious. With their fists raised, they are shouting anti-Chinese slurs. A demonstration is brewing. Yet another one of their colleagues was just attacked by thugs in China. This is becoming a disturbingly common occurrence.

Truck drivers encounter Chinese crime probably more than anyone. They witness it and sometimes experience it, on the supply route between Hong Kong and the mainland. Without produce imported from China, Hong Kong—with its mountainous terrain and a real estate industry devouring the remaining land—would perish. The territory produces very little food. No fruit or vegetables. The little poultry raised is mainly consumed by the farmers themselves on Lantau and other surrounding islands. Trucks, along with trains, are still the fastest means of transportation to supply fresh produce to Hong Kong's 6.2 million inhabitants.

Looking lost among ten or so of his angry colleagues, twenty-seven-year-old Hui Wing-sheung, his arm in a sling, recounts how he was attacked: "It was 3:30 in the afternoon. I was closing the door of my truck when three men, one with a knife, jumped me. They stabbed me in the right forearm and ran off with my wallet."

Highly organized gangs work at three points on the border. The price to pay is usually 500 yuan ($60 US). The triad members operate with impunity, in full view of the Chinese police and customs officials. "You can't help thinking they are accomplices," mutters Hui.

Red with anger, he shouts what many only say to themselves: that the chiefs of the Red Army and the agencies under its auspices—the police and customs—protect and even control the thugs. But no one can prove it.

These latter-day highwaymen are protected by the party officials. The Chinese regime, to be sure, launched a major campaign against corruption in 1996. In the Canton region of the south, not far from Hong Kong, executions have begun taking place. But the problem is profound and endemic.

Truckers are easy prey. They are stuck on the highway for hours and sometimes cannot move until they pass through customs, where the waiting lines are endless.

"The most dangerous place is Man Kam To," says Tung Hwa-din. "It's the entrance with the second-highest amount of traffic. Ten thousand vehicles pass through each day."

Man Kam To closes at 10:00 P.M. and does not reopen until 7:00 A.M. the following day. During the night, while waiting in traffic, truckers are attacked and frequently wounded.

But the truckers refuse to change jobs. They are too well paid. A driver earns between $15,000 to $30,000 HK a month.

A Journalist Loses an Arm

The triads do not hesitate to attack people in the press when they feel their activities are being threatened or if they simply have a contract to fulfill.

In the spring of 1996, on May 15, two men entered the offices of *Surprise* magazine in the neighborhood of Quarry Bay. They said they were typesetters and demanded to see the founding editor-in-chief, Leung Tin-wai. No one paid them any attention. It was layout time, and the editors were busy. In his office, with no witnesses present, the two men cut off one of Leung's thumbs with a razor and slashed off his left forearm with a saber. The magazine was preparing an article on the triads.

Three years before the attack on Leung, the editorial offices of the popular magazine *Next* were ransacked. Not long afterward the owner, Jimmy Lai, one of the press figures most criticized by Beijing, was himself attacked and robbed (see page 91).

Street Urchins, Drug Dealers

Detective Renouf has plenty of stories about the triads. But something that is new is their use of adolescents and even young children. More and more abandoned children and runaways are becoming easy prey for the triads. Statistics show more than two thousand children join triads in a single year. For a few coins they are willing to do anything, for anyone. According to Hong Kong police, many children are used to deliver drugs.

"Minors are usually paid between $200 and $300 HK to carry up to 350 grams of heroin, worth about $300,000 HK," explains Inspector Ip Pau-fuk. The system is simple. The child takes the heroin and hides it in a safe place. Then he leaves a message on his boss's pager, and the boss calls him back to get the address. Nothing could be simpler. Most of the time, the children do not even know they are trafficking drugs.

"We have proof that children of ten and eleven are used as drug couriers," confirms Peter Newbery, director of Youth Outreach. The girls are forced into prostitution, and the boys are recruited by the triads as messengers.

The average age of a young triad member is thirteen. In 1995, a total of three hundred thirty-three youths between the ages of sixteen and twenty were arrested.

Professor Wong Chung-kwong, a psychiatrist, comments: "It's easy to understand why the triads would use children to get their evil merchandise to its destination; they look for a cheap foolproof method! Children are obviously easier to manipulate than adults. And a child in a school uniform doesn't attract the police's attention."

The Triads in the Police

British and proud of it, Detective Renouf is married to a Chinese woman. He has a photo of his children in the place of honor on his desk, between two alarming statistics.

What upsets him most is not when a sting operation fails to catch a shoplifter in the act, but when someone leaks information in his own department. Because the triads are absolutely everywhere, even in the police force.

"What can you do?" he asks, lowering his voice. "I'm not one hundred percent sure of my men's integrity. Several times when we made a raid, the people had obviously been warned. They must have had one or several accomplices among my men, maybe even the ones closest to me. It's the only explanation!"

The British police have all experienced the same problem. It is impossible for them to trust their Chinese colleagues absolutely.

"Drug trafficking involves huge amounts of money—hundreds of thousands, even millions of dollars. How can you stop corruption in the police when some inspectors are only paid a few hundred dollars a month? It's impossible!" says one Officer Wong, a young "untouchable" recently assigned to the Wanchai police headquarters.

So what happens when the last of the British leave? Some British detectives who are under contract will surely stay on for a few years, most of them until the year 2000. But after that—will the triads "redecorate" police headquarters?

A Triad Operation Chart

Tang (an alias) is one of the Hong Kong police's few informers. An uncomplicated man, he proudly sports a multitude of tattoos, midnight-blue dragons with scary-looking tongues, which cover his body.

Roughly twenty years old, he grew up in Tuen Mun, in the New Territories, near the Chinese border. A bedroom suburb with a population of 460,000, it is a place to avoid, a hotbed of delinquency and crime of all types.

1992: A twelve-year-old boy, Ip Kin-kei, was killed by his school friends for refusing to participated in triad activities.

1995: In one month, the residents of the Butterfly Apartments counted no fewer than fifty armed attacks in their building.

These are just two examples. There are dozens more.

Tuen Mun is a dark-gray hell where women do not dare walk alone, even in daylight. It is a pit where no one lives except those who have no other place to go. It is the hidden face of Hong Kong, a forest of housing overlooked by even the most curious tourists.

Tang joined his triad when he was eighteen. His buddies introduced him to friends who knew others.

"I wanted to be in a triad because I thought I would become somebody important," he recounts.

A year after being contacted, he took part in his first operation.

"A street hawker had refused to pay my group on the pretext that he had already paid a hundred dollars to another triad," he says. "To scare him we broke a piece of wood over his head. He never acted up again!"

While in prison, after being convicted of possession of heroin, Tang decided to change. "To help the kids," he says.

"I'm afraid of being found out by the other members," confesses Tang the informer. "But I'll go the whole nine yards. We have to undo the triads and free Hong Kong!" His vow is probably more well-meaning than realistic.

At the top, each triad is organized military-style. The boss is called "Big Brother." To his underlings, he is second only to Buddha. He is the one who initiates new members, with an exchange of blood (reminiscent of Corsican gangs), genuflecting, and an oath of loyalty for life. The lower level is made up of "colonels" and "captains,"al though leaders are identified by numbers rather than ranks. The higher the number, the more powerful the person. A Chief of Combat, for example, is 462, Chief of Liaisons, 432. As for the Grand Master, who bears such poetic names as "Dragon's Head" or "Prince of the Mountain," he is 489, and his assistant is 438. At the bottom of the pyramid is the "Blue Lantern," or the apprentice.

History

What are the triads? An age-old Chinese custom dating back to 1644. After the fall of the Ming Dynasty, five Buddhist monks of the Shaolin Monastery revolted against the Manchus of the Qing Dynasty. They invented martial arts—kung fu—and founded the first triad. Their fight lasted for nearly 400 years, until the founding of the Republic of China by Sun Yat-sen in 1911.

Before the creation of the People's Republic of China, the triads defended Chiang Kai-shek's Nationalists until the latter were defeated and forced into exile in Taiwan and Hong Kong.

Crime was not the triads' original objective. Neither was money. They were secret societies of "mutual aid." Little by little, over the years, they were corrupted by vice, drugs, prostitution—and dirty money.

Today, according to the Royal Hong Kong Police Force, there are roughly sixty triads, with branches throughout Asia.

Three triads dominate the Hong Kong syndicate: Sun Yee-on, the most powerful; 14 K, named after the street of its original meeting place in Canton; and Woh Shing Woh, known under the initials WSW.

These three organizations coexist and even collaborate without many conflicts. They have joint meetings several times a year to divide territories or settle disputes.

No one can say exactly how many members they have. Some estimate that Sun Yee-on's ranks number 56,000. It is impossible to know. They have no permanent members and their organization is very loose. Anyone who wants to work for them can, even on an irregular or temporary basis. A well-placed cousin is enough to get one in.

Drugs, Sex, and Guns

Now that the British are gone, the port of Hong Kong is likely to become the converging point for drugs smuggled from the Golden Triangle (Burma–Laos–Thailand) through the Chinese province of Hunan. The longshoremen, already controlled by the triads, will facilitate transport. Corrupt customs officials will probably look the other way.

However, the triads have concocted an even more ambitious plan. Long before the handover in 1997 they struck a deal with the Japanese gangs, or *yakuza*, for production of the drug 'ice' (which has supplanted heroin) in the Chinese provinces of Fujian, Xiamen, and Guangdong.

The object is simple. Chinese ice will be transported to Europe or the United States aboard freight carriers loaded in Hong Kong.

Likewise, weapons made illegally in the Philippines or China and contraband goods, such as cigarettes and alcohol, will enter the West through the wide open gates of Hong Kong.

"Up to now, we've been working in collaboration with our British colleagues," explains John Daimler, an American investigator. "But now the English aren't there to act as a screen between Asia and the United States." The Hong Kong border will be like a sieve.

Car Theft

The Hong Kong triads also specialize in stealing cars and reselling them in mainland China. They employ state-of-the-art methods which have come a long way since 1993—and, it is said, enjoy the generous cooperation of the Chinese bureaucracy.

Indeed, the situation is tempting. Tantalizing luxury cars crowd Hong Kong's parking lots. Rolls-Royces and Bentleys in gaudy colors—and often exceedingly bad taste—have become a cliche of Hong Kong tourist guidebooks. Mercedes, BMWs and Jaguars abound as well.

As you walk through Hong Kong, you see very few old models, aside from collectors' items. Most of the cars are fresh from the factory.

"In general, a car is old after six months," an amused taxi driver explains. Old does not mean that the car is in bad condition (which is not unlikely, given the island's rough terrain); it simply means that the typical car owner in Hong Kong must always own the latest model to stay ahead of his neighbor—or else there is no point in buying it.

Car thieves go all the way with methods straight out of a police thriller. According to the police, this is the general pattern:

Act I: The thieves are in cahoots with the parking attendants of Kowloon's nightclubs, such as the gigantic China City Night Club, which caters to partying Japanese, or certain big restaurants.

While the unsuspecting car owner is inside enjoying dinner or drinks, copies of his keys are made immediately. Thanks to the cellular telephone, the sale of his car is already being negotiated in mainland China.

Then everything is meticulously planned. The driver of the car is tailed. Quite probably drunk, he does not notice a thing. As soon as he parks in a discrete place, the crooks, equipped with copies of the keys, have only to take possession of the car.

Act II: Ten minutes later, the car is on a boat destined for the Chinese coast, outside of Hong Kong's territorial waters. The cars are usually shipped on outboard motorboats called *tai fei* ("big flies" in Cantonese), which are copies of a Canadian racing model.

For fear of the Chinese Coast Guard, whose officers are noticeably less corrupt than their police colleagues and reputedly trigger-happy, the men who make these trips work very fast and wear bulletproof vests.

Act III: The cars are unloaded on an inlet, which are numerous on the Chinese coast. It is usually done at night, in total secrecy.

The great majority of fishing villages along the Chinese coast live off this business.

"It isn't just cars," explains Yann, a Scottish-born resident who ended up on the island of Hainan about ten years ago. "Household appliances, VCRs, air conditioners, and karaoke equipment are also highly prized."

All this merchandise takes the same route as the cars. They are transported by sea, either in a fast lightweight boat or hidden in a huge freight carrier.

The Hong Kong police regularly seize some of these craft. But how many slip through the net? Hundreds every month, for sure.

The Chinese authorities recognize that this traffic exists. From time to time the official press announces the "return of stolen vehicles to Hong Kong."

On June 3, 1993, the *China Daily* published a report from Canton stating that "eight stolen automobiles had been sent back to the (southern) province of Guangdong in Hong Kong." Most of them, it said, were "luxury cars each worth more than $1 million HK."

Eight cars is a ridiculously low figure, given the uninterrupted flow of high-performance Mercedes and Toyota Crowns unloaded in China.

"In addition to the security all along the border," the Chinese newspaper declared, "the government of Guangdong has refused to register automobiles with the steering wheel on the right, because it is likely that they were stolen in Hong Kong." This is a minor masterpiece of disingenuousness: Where else would these vehicles come from, and how else would they have landed in China, where people drive on the right side of the road?

PROSTITUTION

Good-bye Suzy Wong

142 Prince Edward Road West is a six-floor concrete building from the 1950s, an ordinary gray and blue low-income housing complex. And yet, behind the barred windows sits the strategic center of the war on crime in Hong Kong.

Across from the Prince Edward subway station, less than an hour from mainland China, stands the police station. It is in the heart of the Mongkok quarter's maze of squalid alleys, ablaze with multicolored neon signs and crawling with coolies and peddlers, a labyrinth grazed by the wings of the Boeing planes landing in Hong Kong.

Drugs, prostitution, blackmail, corruption, fraud of all kinds, and clandestine workshops are rife. The quarter smells of fried tofu.

On the third floor at the end of a maze of corridors with light blue walls is the office of the District Operation Officer, John Fraser. The decor is classic "cop"—a blackboard to explain the dragnets to his men, a tea kettle, and a computer.

At thirty-two, Fraser supervises six teams of police officers, each headed by an inspector and two sergeants. They are Hong Kong's version of the "Untouchables."

John Fraser is English. He received his training at Scotland Yard before being appointed here. Dark, well-built, single, but rather shy and awkward, dressed like a schoolboy who grew up too quickly, he is no James Bond. His targets are the vice establishments and places of debauchery. When he speaks, he spares no details; you would think he is giving a tour of his village neighborhood.

"In Hong Kong," he explains, "there's hardly any prostitution in the street. No street walkers, with the exception of a moving population of nonprofessionals who increase their monthly earnings on Saturday night in the Wanchai quarter."

Leila is nineteen. Like many of her coworkers, she comes from the mainland—Canton, in her case.

"Money," she declares, "is the only thing that counts in China. Big bucks . . . if you do not have any, you can't survive. There's no way! So, I came here. Later, I'll go to Macao." In 1999 the Portuguese will hand over the keys of that city to the Chinese, two years after the Hong Kong reversion.

Leila speaks Cantonese, the Hong Kong dialect, which gives her a distinct advantage over other Chinese prostitutes from the north who speak only Mandarin, a language understood by few in the territory.

Leila is quite attractive despite her "uniform" consisting of spike heels and leather mini-skirt. The main tool of her trade is the mobile phone.

The Villas, or, Karaokes for Special Parties

Leila is in constant contact with a procurer, a *ma foo*—a Cantonese word for stable boy. She spends her evenings waiting for the phone to ring, never leaving her neighborhood. She does not go to the client; he comes to her, through her *ma foo*.

To find these villas, you only need to wander the area near the Jordan subway station and follow the signs. In general, for reasons unknown, these "villas" flourish near markets. You can take your pick. A client names his preference: Thai, Chinese, young, old, fat, ugly—there is someone to suit any taste. It is like a rummage sale of sex.

Hong Kong, however, is not Bangkok. Here the client cannot window shop for women, as in Thailand, where women are literally displayed with an identification number. In a Hong Kong "villa" the client must trust the owner. Like Leila, who is waiting on the line, he, too, must wait patiently with a cup of tea—the only thing that is free—while they come up with his dream girl.

The price? Between $300 and $500 HK for "a moment."

"Our main problem," Fraser explains, "is the importation of prostitutes. As the months roll by, more and more illegal prostitutes are coming from People's China. The number has tripled in two years. The largest number come from mainland."

In 1994, according to Royal Police statistics, in the Mongkok quarter alone, which has 100,000 inhabitants, "only" 415 prostitutes were mainlanders. The following year, 967 were counted. One Chinese prostitute per one hundred inhabitants, in addition to prostitutes from Thailand, the Philippines, and Malaysia.

Sometimes Leila takes part in orgies at swingers' parties in special night clubs, euphemistically dubbed "karaokes." In theory, people come to karaokes to drink, listen to the music, and sing along with a star on a video. In reality, many of these clubs, very much the rage in Asia, are disguised vice establishments, equipped with very discreet and extremely private salons. Behind the curtains nothing is seen or heard.

Massage Parlors

"And of course, like everywhere else," Fraser relates, "there are 'specialized' massage parlors. Most are thinly disguised houses of prostitution." The seediest ones are downtown, in the Central or Wanchai quarters. Only the poorest go there, or people looking for a "quickie." They can be spotted by their "candy canes," the gyrating red and blue cylinders usually found in front of barbershops.

At the entrance—in the old buildings, usually at the top of the stairs—a chubby Buddha with his traditional red lantern is enthroned, enveloped in an opaque smoke from a few incense sticks. Images of this divinity are everywhere in Hong Kong, even in places of debauchery.

Loretta is originally from the Philippines. Plump, unattractive, disheveled, she is a masseuse at one of the salons located on Lie Yuen Street West, between Queen's Road and Des Voeux Road. Her workplace looks much like any other salon.

In the semi-darkness of a dismal room, barely lit by a few red lightbulbs, the clients are seated, fully dressed, one next to the other in authentic barber chairs. The room looks like a barbershop scene in a B-movie. The clothes on hangers suspended from the ceiling belong to the masseuses. This is also where they live. When there are no clients, they take turns sleeping on the massage "tables." The prostitutes from the mainland did not flee People's China for political reasons, but in the hopes of getting rich. Once they arrived in Hong Kong they stayed with cousins, looking for work. But without papers they searched in vain, and eventually wound up in the sex trade. Their salary? Whatever their triad bosses want to pay, usually roughly the equivalent of $1,000 US a month for 10 clients a day.

"Within twenty-four hours they earn more in a month than secretaries in Canton," John Higgers points out. He is a client of Loretta's, whom she met in a bar. A friendly Texan in his fifties, he came to Hong Kong to slum around.

"The actual massage lasts about ten minutes," he explains. "The session usually ends in masturbation." The price is $300 HK.

Other parlors are more sophisticated and more expensive. They offer a whole range of treatments: sauna, shower, pool bathing, manicures and pedicures. These deluxe parlors advertise their services on neon signs, like the "Diamond Palace Sauna," for example, in the Wanchai quarter. Their prices are high. It all depends on the "service." Service with sex costs $1,500 HK.

There are similar places for women, which are more discreet, more expensive, and more luxurious. Many are on the other side of the border in People's China. A nightclub in Shenzhen, a tea-dancing salon of sorts, with bedrooms upstairs, is frequented by youths, gigolos, and women of a certain age. Tycoons' wives, in general.

Gays and lesbians have their parlors as well. The "Propaganda" bar is one. A complete list of them would fill a telephone book.

Call Girls, Brothels, and Fish Balls

Hong Kong's rich take advantage of the services of call girls. You need only open any general news daily written in Chinese to find an unbelievable number of ads. Most popular newspapers offer them, as well as the more serious ones.

Imagine leafing through the *Times* of London or the *New York Times* and finding, sandwiched between two articles on Bosnia, full-color ads for prostitutes, complete with photos. Japanese women are usually advertised, for they are in the highest demand—not only for their professional qualities, but for historical reasons as well.

Hong Kong men, who are known to be macho, have a reputation

for mistreating women in general and prostitutes in particular. They also have not forgotten the Japanese occupation of China from 1937 to 1945. They believe they are exacting a measure of revenge whenever they use Japanese prostitutes.

As in most cities, the practical and discreet brothels are frequented by the bourgeois class. A parking space closes and the client is escorted directly to the bar where the girls are waiting.

Finally, the "most sordid sites," according to detectives, are the "fish-ball stalls," where "fish-ball" vendors offer behind-the-counter oral sex by elderly prostitutes at cut-rate prices. The action takes place in total darkness behind a curtain at the back of the stall.

"In general, we can't catch them in the act," explains Fraser, "None of my men would go near those places because the women are so old!"

The Wanchai Bars: Goodbye Suzy Wong

Hong Kong bars are not what they used to be. At Hot Lips on Lockhart Road, or at the nearby Neptune, Suzy Wong has disappeared for good. By the end of the 1980s, the superbly full-lipped Chinese girls in slit skirts reluctantly deserted the Wanchai quarter bars, seeking refuge in the posh karaokes and the massage parlors for millionaires on the binge. Competition was too strong.

Today's barflies are Filipino or Thai. Unemployed young girls, many without visas, agree to twist and shake a few inches in front of customers for a measly salary. Barely out of school, they dance topless in a semicircle facing a mirror on top of the bar. It is a pathetic show, like a train station snack bar at closing time on a Monday. Here is the Third World lit up on a neon dance-floor.

The girls, many who are gorgeous, do what they can to catch the eye of a passing sailor. But it is no erotic encounter. Poorly stuffed into thick nylon pantyhose up to the waist, they seem distant, in search of a handout just to buy a bowl of rice with sauce.

In the same neighborhood, at the Country Club, the dancers are more aggressive, wearing metal chains and bottomless leather pants. It is the same scene everywhere: the client is asked to buy a drink for one of the "artists" by the mamasan on duty, the lady pimp, who is usually a Filipino.

Usually that is about as far as an encounter goes. If a regular client insists on more, he must pay a hefty exit fee to take the girl out of the club. Afterward, anything can be negotiated.

After 4:00 A.M. at the New Pussy Cat, on Fenwick Street, it is a different story. The atmosphere is more amicable. Dancers show up like neighbors for one last drink, looking for an easy drunk to roll. But there are also the maids, off duty for a few hours, who come to listen to disco music. Here the mamasan is called Bernadette. The night owls and foreign journalists know this voluptuous, fortyish Filipino woman well. She graciously makes sure that her clients are treated well, without ever pushing drinks on anyone. Everyone mingles— servicemen on leave, businessmen, and lonely diplomats. The women dance their hearts out. The drinks are affordable. It is probably the only place in Hong Kong where everyone finds what her or she was looking for—dancing, a little company, or a one-night stand.

POVERTY

A Pocket of Resistance

Hong Kong is a world of black and white extremes, a universe of brutal antagonisms. In a flash, you jump from one world to another. From the superficial and transitory to jealously preserved traditions. Skyscrapers of rose granite and dark steel with silver or gold windows in the Central quarter stand in contrast to the rundown slums of the commercial quarter in Wanchai. The sharp angles and shapes of ultra-modern buildings, the blinking neon signs at night, and the deafening noise of the city are a counterpoint to the small remote alleyways of the New Territories or Victoria Peak's meandering hillside paths. The fast vedettes of the Aberdeen Marina know nothing of the old dusty skiffs which crowd and pollute the main port.

The rich are enormously rich. They have amassed unbelievable fortunes which they flaunt at every turn. The tycoons live in marble palaces, drive Rolls, wear diamond watches, dress in Hermès, sail on yachts. Their wives, their *taitai*, spend the better part of their time pampering themselves in beauty centers imported from France, window-shopping in deluxe shops such as Cartier or Chanel, or traveling throughout the world in first class.

The poor, on the other hand, are deplorably poor. Poverty reaches unimaginable depths within such a flashy jewel box as Hong Kong. Near the old Kai Tak Airport the impoverished live in "cages."

The Cages

In staircases strewn with garbage, the nauseating smell of rancid duck fat stings your throat. You can get a tour of these notorious "cages," on the third floor of a building in the Mongkok quarter, hardly five subway stops from the center of Hong Kong, one of the richest places in the world.

Humanitarian groups such as Oxfam, a private organization, are taking journalists on tours around the lower depths of Hong Kong. Today's group includes a handful of photographers and an Australian television crew. The show is pathetic and revolting. The cameras flash. The foreigners are embarrassed and vaguely guilty. They feel like voyeurs.

The cages? That is what all Hong Kong calls them. In truth, no other word fits.

Lung Mai-hun, sixty-four years old, is dressed simply in a filthy

T-shirt and slacks. "I've lived here for twenty-four years," he says, smiling. "It's my home. I don't want to leave." Behind the thick bars installed by the owners, Lung, like the other renters, has a living space of roughly one and a half by two meters. Barely enough room to lay down a gutted mattress and nail a few shelves to the wall. It is impossible to stand up straight. In his building each room is divided into six cages. There are three rooms on each floor.

Lung, who was born in Shanghai, is not the only one hanging onto his cage. There are several thousand—nearly three thousand, according to official figures, ten thousand, according to humanitarian organizations—living this way, well below the poverty line recognized by international organizations. These people are either those who were "lost in the shuffle during the boom," or those "who never caught a break"—any cliché will do.

The vast majority are old Chinese immigrants who fled communism after 1949. Most have small jobs as peddlers, selling anything for an average salary of $300 HK per month ($40 US).

"I make out," explains Lung. "My rent for the cage comes to $43 HK ($6 US) per month. I can even help out my grandchildren."

It is so pitiful to see his smiling, emaciated, toothless face behind these bars!

The British have certainly tried, though with no great urgency and thus far unsuccessfully, to house these unfortunate people. As soon as they empty the cages, they fill up again.

During the last few years, 150 mainland Chinese have been permitted to emigrate to Hong Kong each day. With no place to spend their first night, many were pleased to find a few square meters to squat—and many of them have stayed on.

Declining Consumerism

The cages illustrate the deep gap between the fabulously rich and the desperately poor. In Hong Kong, 650,000 people, or 9% of the population, are poor. This number has doubled in the past six years.

The Chinese newspaper *Ming Bao* published a survey conducted in 1994 and 1995 on 72,000 unmarried people in Hong Kong. It found:

44% had only $525 HK ($70 US) per month to feed themselves
40% had $483 ($63 US) per month for housing

1995 saw a clear drop in consumption. The first reason was the skyrocketing price of real estate. The people of Hong Kong bought fewer and fewer goods in order to pay their rent. Another reason for the drop was a significant rise in unemployment, to 3.2% of the population. Compared to the rest of the world, particularly industrialized Western nations, 3.2% is enviably low. Nonetheless, consumer confidence was also low, as the population spent less due to worries about the future. Durable goods, in particular, suffered, as some people prepared for the possibility of having to leave Hong Kong in a hurry.

Living on Three Dollars a Day

During the often cold winter months the media remind us regularly about the plight of the elderly, left to fend for themselves in lonely and often wretched conditions. Thirty thousand senior citizens receive the minimum pension of $25 HK a day, roughly $3 US.

Mr. Yao, seventy-four, lives on Prince Road in a six-square-meter room and has received this standard allowance for the past thirteen years. He has no kitchen, so he uses his rice cooker as both a stove and a refrigerator by filling it with ice water.

At noon Mr. Yao eats in the street. A plate of rice mixed with tofu comes to $22 HK. In the evening he heats up a quarter can of pork, which costs $5.50 HK a can. He smokes cigarettes, which cost him $500 HK a month.

Mrs. Ng Xiao Feng, seventy-five, lives in Da Heng Village, on the eighth floor of a building without an elevator. She goes to the market every day, which takes half an hour on foot, for its bargain prices. Mrs. Xiao Feng has her rules. She keeps nothing in the refrigerator and will not reheat leftovers, to save on gas and electricity. She prefers salted vegetables because they are inexpensive, filling, and keep for a long time.

China for the Chinese

All the people left by the wayside of Hong Kong's boom are quite pleased by the arrival of their "cousins" from People's China. At any rate, their lot could hardly get any worse. Most fled communism in 1949 but have not struck it rich. So they hope that the Communists will ultimately do more than the colonial government did to improve their situation, even though the British had set up a series of rather successful programs.

Li is a taxi driver. On the windshield of his red, white-roofed Toyota hangs a photograph of Mao Zedong.

"I'm delighted to see the British get out," he says. "This is China we're in and it is about time that we live among our own people!"

This idea of giving back "China to the Chinese" is making inroads among the poor. The Communists in charge should beware. If they do not take rapid measures to improve the conditions of life for the poorest, the poor could well revolt. They are hoping for even more from their communist countrymen than from the English. This is a pocket of potential anti-Beijing resistance not to be ignored.

RACISM

Immigrants Have a Short Memory

Historically, Hong Kong has been the temple of immigration, probably the most sought-after asylum in Asia over the last century.

The island has welcomed famous refugees: the Vietnamese Ho Chi

Minh, as well as Sun Yat-sen, the founding father of the Chinese Republic in his struggle against the Manchurian Dynasty. In the aftermath of World War II, it was the "rock" where thousands came to seek their fortunes. In the ten years after 1945, twenty thousand Europeans passed through Hong Kong.

Most of them were White Russians who fled the Soviet Union in the 1920s to seek asylum in China. There were also Spanish, Greek, and Austrian expatriates who worked on the construction of the Manchurian railway. After the occupation of the Province by the Soviet Union in 1945, they fled yet again.

Hicks with a Knack for Business

Of course, Hong Kong represented the "bridge of hope" for thousands of Chinese after the Communist victory over Chiang Kai-shek's Nationalists in 1949. An agreement between the Chinese and the English at the time permitted fifty people per day to cross over the border. Nevertheless, during the next 10 years, the flow of illegal aliens swelled to 90,000 per year. In 1962, due to political conditions and economic disasters in China, the pace increased: 500,000 people tried to seek refuge in the colony; half were turned away.

Hong Kong is overflowing with immigrants or sons of immigrants from People's China, many originally from the southern coastal regions of Shanghai or Canton. Hundreds of them are proud to recall that they amassed gigantic fortunes after having landed with only a few dollars in their pockets. They arrived after the proclamation of the People's Republic of China or later, after the terrible years of the Cultural Revolution (1966–1976).

Through hard work, zeal, and willpower they managed to carve out comfortable lives for themselves in Hong Kong. The wealthiest drive around in Rolls Royces, dress in Lanvin and awkwardly gulp down cognac from gold-corked bottles.

However, the majority of Hong Kong's tycoons are illiterate, uncultured men with a knack for business, who benefited from the under-development and cheap manual labor in their native land. How many of these *nouveau riches* are able to swear under oath that they did not get rich selling products assembled by children on the mainland? Probably none.

In any case, rare are those in Hong Kong who have used their wealth for humanitarian or charitable causes. The worst of it is that these former immigrants are full of cynicism and a surprising preju-dice toward new arrivals who, like them fifty years ago, are seeking a better life today. A survey published in 1997 by the local press indi-cated that the majority of Hong Kong's residents consider the main-land Chinese newcomers ignorant, dirty, and vulgar. And they let them know it every day, always distrusting and sometimes humiliat-ing them.

Hatred for Newcomers

Fung Man-chen, forty years old, arrived in Hong Kong from Canton in 1995. Now, working as a small hand in the printing business, he still has difficulties trying to fit into the local life. Fung lives with his two children, two and ten years old, in Shamshuipo, in the New Ter-ritories, a common quarter known for selling pirated copies of com-puter programs.

"I think I'm a victim of discrimination," he explains. "I do not understand why they hate the mainland Chinese so much. We're all Chinese! Before coming here, I thought I was going to have a bright future in Hong Kong. I speak Cantonese so I do not have any lan-guage problem. I was realistic. I knew it wasn't going to be easy to get rich, but I thought that I could make it by working hard. I never could have imagined all the obstacles that I would encounter coming from the people themselves."

How, why does he feel rejected?

"I've tried to find a school for my son. We kept trying for five or six months, but everyone sent us about our business when they found out we were immigrants. The usual excuse to push us aside was to pretend that the educational level in People's China was lower than Hong Kong's, especially in English. My son's neither stupid nor illiterate. He studied a lot in Canton and is perfectly capable of working as hard as necessary to raise his level. We've perhaps finally found a school, thanks to the help of a social worker."

What is the main problem encountered by Mr. Fung in Hong Kong?

"Housing. Rents are very high. I earn about $6,000 HK per month and the rent for the room where we live costs me more than one third of my funds. I can't feed my children properly with this expense. It would be good if the government would give us priority for social housing."

There are thousands of Chinese victims of discrimination like him.

Disgusted, some choose to return to mainland China where, in extreme cases, they commit suicide. In 1995 there was a 3.6% increase in suicides from the previous year's figure.

The charity organization Good Samaritans is made up of volunteers who speak fifteen different languages, including three Chinese dialects. These volunteers answer the telephones twenty-four hours a day to help the desperate. The Good Samaritans received 20,519 phone calls during the year 1995–96, 13.5% more than in 1994.

The yearly report by this organization points out that in 1996: "Suicide is not linked to age, group, or a specific ethnic group, but it is important to note that in 1995 . . . 429 of those who committed suicide were out of work. This census revealed that 82% are Chinese, whereas there were only 62% in 1989."

Why are these mainland Chinese so disliked by the Chinese of Hong Kong? Undoubtedly, it has more to do with the class struggle rather than ethnic reasons. The people of Hong Kong denigrate the new-comers from mainland China for their poverty. As soon as the elite have a few coins in their pockets they feel superior to their "brothers" from People's China. Money has made them lose their sense of morality as well as their memory.

This refusal to help the poorest to adapt can also be seen in the scandalous way the people of Hong Kong "welcome" immigrants who have arrived from other downtrodden Asian countries, especially those coming from the Philippines.

"Little Maids"

In Spain during the 1960s, to earn a living in Franco's Andalusia you had to be either a *guardia civil* or a bullfighter. Today, Philippine women emigrating to Hong Kong have to be either housemaids or prostitutes. There are no other options.

Rosario, age twenty-five, chose the first solution. She works in the home of a rich importer of Chinese furniture. "Even if you find work in the Philippines," she explains, "you do not earn enough money to feed your family. A doctor at home earns as much as domestic help here! So. . . ."

So, planeloads of them leave the islands of their dreams in the hopes of being hired in Hong Kong. Many of them have degrees. It does not matter—they prefer being maids to the alternative.

They are regularly taken advantage of by middlemen.

"Hong Kong is a city of vice, drugs, and dirty money. Not one for honest working girls!" Saying this, old Chang snickers into the palm of his hand. He runs one of the many "placement agencies" that have multiplied in the small streets around Queen's Road. His mistress is from the Philippines. She is thirty-five years his junior. As his tout, she takes a month's salary from the new recruits, whose numbers grow each day.

"A lot of them end up in prostitution," Chang laments. "They earn a lot more in less time!"

Slave Drivers

The majority of women, who persevere and refuse to fall into vice, send the lion's share of their salaries to their families in the Philippines. Many have children which they had to abandon, as immigrants from all developing nations have had to do.

Living conditions for the Filipinos are miserable. There are only two solutions: the fortunate ones end up working for foreigners, the others are employed by Chinese who are, for the most part, overbearing and racist.

"In the middle of the night, my Shanghai master woke me up to cook for him," states Maria. "Routinely, no matter what time it is, often four in the morning, I have to set the table and wait on him. I have to wait until he's finished. I must satisfy his slightest wish. Sometimes massage him or wash his feet. But I'm not the worst off: I have some friends who have to get into bed with their employers or else it is out the door!"

Rosario's view of the Chinese is even harsher. "The Chinese from here are often immensely rich but they do not have any education. They belch, pick their teeth . . . I'll leave out the details. They're vulgar people. I've been here for four years, but I can't get used to it."

In the bourgeois buildings of Mid Levels or the rich hills of Victoria Peak, the maids' rooms are incredibly narrow, demonstrating their employers' disregard for their welfare. Some living spaces are too small to even fit a bed. The girls sleep curled up on makeshift mattresses as if they were living in the nineteenth century.

The ever-smiling maids earn $4,000 HK per month. The employer draws up a contract, countersigned by the Immigration Service of Hong Kong. The women are "housed" and fed, and get a day off every Sunday. They use it to gather together.

A One-of-a-Kind Show

Every Sunday—the "Lord's day," as Rosario calls it—Central, the business district, offers a one-of-a-kind show. Usually filled with busy white-collar workers, the place undergoes a metamorphosis: it becomes human. You only need to listen how their voices blend, how they chat and ramble on like the hum of air conditioning.

They meet by the tens of thousands at the foot of the skyscrapers, symbols of the territory's wealth. While the golden boys are at the beach, the hired help take to the streets. It is as if Wall Street were suddenly transformed into Woodstock!

In 1995 there were 131,165 domestic workers from the Philippines, according to the official census. After Manila, Hong Kong has the largest Filipino community of the world. Not one of these Filipino women, who are of all ages, would miss these Sunday meetings. It is a ritual, their weekly joy, and favorite pastime. Their connection to friends from home.

In front of the Kowloon ferry wharf, across from the deserted Stock Exchange, or on the asphalt of Des Voeux Road closed to traffic, they sit on the ground on blankets, rain or shine. One of them has brought her guitar, the other has baked a cake. They are pretty, fun-loving, loud, and friendly. Their ages range from twenty to fifty-five. They are full-lipped with teasing looks and smooth, black hair. There are hardly any men to be seen. Between outbursts of laughter, the women show each other photos of fiancés or husbands back home, reminisce about their village, or share the latest rumors from their island. They chatter away like they would at home.

They all speak English perfectly well. But here on the sidewalks among fellow countrywomen they speak only their native tongue, Tagalog.

People's China? They could not care less. They hope, as they read in the newspapers, that "for the next fifty years nothing will change."

El Shaddai

In the meantime, they find comfort where they can.

"A lot of the girls are homosexual," explains John Hamilton, a university professor whose specialty is ethnic minorities. "But the vast majority of these extremely religious women belong to a sect, 'El Shaddai,' a Hebrew word which means God."

Following the precepts of a guru is, in effect, often their only way to keep going. Their guru is fifty-eight-year old Mariano Velarde, or "Brother Mike." He is a favorite of the Filipino women, and not only in Hong Kong. In Manila, El Shaddai regularly organizes meetings of more than 100,000 people in a vacant lot behind the international convention center.

Mariano Velarde, decked out in a flashy jacket, a frilled shirt, and gaudy shoes, looks like a European pimp. He is an American-style preacher who professes a Catholicism adapted to Asian materialism.

"If you love God," he declares, "you will become rich and powerful." He speaks a language that reaches his followers.

"Do you want a refrigerator?" he recently asked during a meeting in Hong Kong. "If you believe in God, you'll have one."

The love these Philippine women have for this folksy appeal reveals the extent of their loneliness. "Brother Mike" is their thoughtmaster.

"He could ask us to do anything," sums up Maria, proud of her loyalty.

El Shaddai has 600,000 followers. Filipino domestics in Hong Kong and elsewhere regularly wire him money. Brother Mike denies being dishonest, however.

"I'm a pickpocket," he answers by fits and starts. "I do not steal money, I extract souls from Satan's claws!"

The Vietnamese Boat People

It is difficult to paint a full picture of Hong Kong, and of the vulgarity and racism of its inhabitants , without recalling the Vietnamese tragedy, hardly a point of pride for the people of Hong Kong.

Beginning in 1975, thousands of boat people fled Vietnam, some for political reasons, but most for economic ones, and came ashore to Hong Kong after terrible weeks on rough seas. History repeats itself. These Vietnamese found themselves in conditions of poverty and weakness identical to those the majority of Chinese found themselves in some thirty years earlier.

Alas, the people of Hong Kong have a short memory. Instead of extending a helping hand to these refugees, who, like them, were seeking a new start in life, they mistreated the Vietnamese in the worst possible way.

Life in the territory was healthy. The island was experiencing an economic boom. Gold was flowing and business flourishing. Buildings were springing up at a rapid pace and construction companies were short of labor. The Hong Kong Chinese, who had suddenly become wealthy, and badly needed construction workers, could have easily integrated these Vietnamese people, who were like themselves three decades earlier, who had braved sharks and storms aboard nutshells on the South China Sea in hopes of building a better life. The Chinese did not rise to the occasion; on the contrary, they rejected the refugees.

The Vietnamese were locked up like criminals in prison camps, mostly unsanitary, decrepit temporary barracks or abandoned factories.

Integration never occurred. The Vietnamese could not blend into the population, let alone find a common language. As soon as they landed, they were questioned, arrested and jailed. They were refused the most basic medical care.

In the September 1996 issue of *Le Temps stratégique*, Derek Maitland, founder of *Hope*, a newspaper published in both English and Vietnamese, testified:

Information leaks have brought to our attention (in 1978) that dozens of babies died in camps because of lack of medical care. Their parents were refused permission by the Chinese guards to go to the hospital. We've checked and double-checked this information; it is obvious to us that these children didn't get sick during the sea crossing, since most died several weeks, even several months, after their arrival. I finally got an appointment with David Wilson, who was a political advisor for the government at the time, and was later to become governor. He explained to me, quite frankly, that the official policy was, indeed, to make life 'uncomfortable' for the Vietnamese in Hong Kong. I use his term so as to discourage the arrival of new refugees. Naturally, he says he's dismayed to learn about the babies who died.

No one in Hong Kong lifted a finger to assist the thousands of families penned in pitiful conditions, imprisoned without communication with the outside world. Their only crime was their wish to flee Vietnam's misery and corruption.

Little by little, these boat people have been deported. In 1995 and 1996 they climbed onto the roofs of their prisons, they burned furniture, screaming out their agony. To no avail. Their desperate revolt was brought down by clubbings, beatings, and tear gas. With the exception of a handful of political agitators that Hanoi did not want to take back, the vast majority of these unfortunate people were sent back to their homeland by chartered planeloads, against their will and without discussion. The rate of these "deportations" accelerated late in 1996 because the Chinese of People's China did not want to hear about the refugees. They demanded that the English "get rid of" this cumbersome population before the handover of Hong Kong on June 30, 1997.

Over the years, the Vietnamese tragedy has gone on amidst general indifference. The camps were "cleaned up" in less than two years without arousing the slightest indignation of the people of Hong Kong. Only the press has given the Vietnamese any attention, in the form of a few news articles.

The Respectable Face

Hong Kong's Future Linked with Beijing's

Hong Kong is one of the world's richest territories, the center of Chinese foreign trade, and the broker of foreign investments in the People's Republic of China. With only 6.2 million inhabitants, compared to China's 200 million, Hong Kong's economic output equals about 1/4 of China's. Its per capita gross domestic product (GDP) is $25,000 US—a level close to that of France, a country with ten times the population and an incomparably rich history.

The reason for this success? The splendid work of its inhabitants, an extremely dynamic voluntary work force in its prime. In 1945 Hong Kong was hardly more than a rock, populated by a modest six hundred thousand inhabitants; now it boasts the seventh most important stock market in the world. It holds the world's fifth largest monetary reserves, as well as the fifth largest foreign-exchange market.

In 1997, the first post-British budget, put forth by Secretary of Finance David Tsang, provided for a 5.5% rise in GDP, an 8% rise in exports of services, an 8.5% rise in exports of goods, and a 5.5% rise in consumption. The prestigious World Economic Forum estimates that Hong Kong is on the verge of taking second place among the most competitive economies of the world.

To what can we attribute these feats? Partly to Hong Kong's laissez-faire economic system, and partly to the value of its currency, the Hong Kong dollar, which has remained pegged to the US dollar, ensuring financial stability. These accomplishments can also be explained by the care the government has taken to avoid favoring Hong Kong investments over foreign investments. All companies involved in public services, including transportation, telephone, electricity, and gas, are private companies which have reinvested their profits into the economy. The authorities have not sought to nationalize them.

And finally—obviously—Hong Kong has benefited from its exceptional geographic position, as a veritable bridge between the West and China.

Relocation of the Industrial Sector to China

In ten years Hong Kong has completely reinvented itself. Since the late 1980s this territory, scarcely the size of metropolitan London, has done away with about a million industrial jobs, and gradually relocated 90% of its industrial equipment across the border to mainland China. The colony shut down its (sometimes clandestine) workshops, where workers slaved night and day, often in subhuman conditions. The workshops were relocated to the mainland, where they have benefited from notably lower rents. Operation costs have dropped considerably. Hong Kong has managed this grafting while maintaining a low unemployment rate of 2.5%. It has simultaneously created jobs in various branches of the service sector.

In one stroke, with no major jolts to its social stability, Hong Kong changed from an industrial economy to a service economy. As Philippe Aguignier of the Parisbas Group in Hong Kong points out: "Fifteen years ago, in a way, Hong Kong lived with its back turned to China. Today the interlocking of the economies of Hong Kong and China is complete."

As soon as Beijing opened its economy to foreign investors in the 1970s, Hong Kong businessmen were at the front of the line. They rushed in, which strongly encouraged the integration of Hong Kong's economy with China's, and contributed to the economic modernization of China.

In spite of the Chinese authorities' desperate desire to promote Shanghai as an international financial center, it is in Hong Kong where Chinese enterprises have raised and continue to raise capital. 75% of China's international financing is done in Hong Kong. Foreign investors prefer by far to do business in Hong Kong rather than in China because of the quality of Hong Kong's legal system. Unlike Hong Kong's, Chinese law is archaic, obscure, and confusing.

Today, half of the foreign investments in China, estimated at $30 billion US annually, come from Hong Kong. More than 60% of China's foreign trade passes through its port, which, with Singapore, has one of the highest levels of freight traffic in the world. In the banking sector, 41% of Hong Kong's dollars located abroad are found in China.

All of these statistics confirm a basic truth: If you are interested in Hong Kong's future, you must be informed about China's as well.

Which is to say, if Beijing airs out its political system, if it modernizes its economic apparatus, as it has begun to do, the future of Hong Kong should be prosperous. On the other hand, if China suffers political or economic upheavals, it is impossible to imagine that Hong Kong will remain as rich and stable as is today.

Last but not least, there is still one major unknown—politics.

If Hong Kong poses the slightest threat to Beijing's communist regime, it is a sure thing that Beijing will resort to reprisals—and the confidence of international investors will gradually fade. Hong Kong will become an island once again. So, in the immediate future—a bet on Hong Kong is a bet on China.

In fact, the People's Republic of China has already invaded Hong Kong's economy through intermediaries. An article in the *Asian Wall Street Journal* of January 30, 1977 points out that China has progressively put "quasi-nationalization" into play in Hong Kong. The key sectors are surrounded—suffocated?—by a proliferating breed of "red tycoons." Capitalists close to Beijing are firmly holding the reigns of Hong Kong's economy.

THE ECONOMY

From the twenty-ninth floor of his spacious office building, Zhang Dachun contemplates his empire with relish. Most of the cargo passing by, like tiny black playing pieces in a floating game of dominoes, belongs to him.

Who is Mr. Zhang? The president of the Cosco Group Limited, a Hong Kong-based maritime freight company founded in 1984, which employs 6,000 people. It is an exclusively Chinese capitalist group.In fourteen years his fleet has become a giant, the second largest in the territory. At this rate, Cosco no doubt will soon be the largest in Hong Kong.

This multimillionaire, a pleasant man, is one of the countless Chinese tycoons, friends of Beijing's, who populate the economic and financial landscape of Hong Kong—and have done so for quite some time.

China actually awakened to the anticipated change in sovereignty several years ago. As soon as they opened their market in the late 1970s, Chinese investors wisely pitched their tent in the colony.

Beijing's Friends Discovered El Dorado in the Late 1970s

The "mainlanders," as Hong Kong's residents call them, to distinguish themselves from the Chinese, could not wait until midnight of July 1, 1997 to put down roots in the territory. That night, the raising of the red flag on the city's public buildings merely confirmed an already well-established presence. Long before that moment, the friends of Beijing had picked up the scent of money. Thousands toed the mark and sprinted south to discover El Dorado.

As early as the nineteenth century many clans already had small branches of their family businesses in Hong Kong. But these businesses were small in scale. As 1997 approached, sharp-minded Chinese with Community Party connections shifted into high gear. These hardened gamblers realized that by combining their powerful friendships in Chinese politics with the realities of Western business, they had an explosive combination—and a major source of money.

Hong Kong offered them a respectable window on the world, the ideal bridge between communism and capitalism, the dreamed-of means of becoming an enormous offshore banking and financial center.

Most of them started with hardly any equipment and only a handful of employees. No problem: once they got going they made inestimable fortunes. From 1977 to 1997 the communists landed. Instead of guns they were armed with datebooks, purchase orders, cellular telephones, and wills of iron.

Their strongest asset was, naturally, the huge demand in the West for cheaply manufactured goods. But also—perhaps more important—their *guanxi*, or contacts in the upper echelons of the Chinese government, were highly coveted by Westerners. In Communist China it is impossible to get through Chinese customs and its bureaucratic labyrinth without some serious inside help. It is likewise impossible to obtain competitive prices from plant managers, and therefore impossible to guarantee shipments on time. *Guanxi* makes China run. Without it, there is no business, and no profits.

A visible example of one of the little gifts which have been typical of corruption on both sides of the border for decades is the magnificent, brand-new Hong Kong branch of China's Ministry of

Foreign Affairs. It was built and graciously offered to Beijing by
Li Ka-shing, one of the island's most influential "red tycoons" (see
page 71).

Over the course of years, then, Deng Xiaoping's reforms have
merrily crossed the Pearl River. Chinese money has invaded Hong
Kong. A string of small Chinese businesses has risen to the heights
of the dragons of Indonesia or Singapore.

"Red Companies" Open Public Relations Offices

"Red" enterprises that formerly fled from publicity—by necessity,
under communism—have opened public relations offices. In 1992,
in the Central district, the labyrinthine commercial area, one concrete building was sold for the astronomical price of $493.5 million.
The newcomers, a group of Chinese businessmen, paid their real
estate agent a commission of $18 million without blinking. Sunshine
Properties, a company directed by a variety of high-ranking figures,
including one mayor, comes from the southern mainland province
of Guangdong, two hours by train from Hong Kong.

Today the blinding neon logos of Chinese businesses shine from
atop the skyscrapers of Des Voeux Road, Queen's Road, and other
thoroughfares of Central. The local office of the Bank of China is
housed in a magnificent glass-and-steel tower in the form of stylized
bamboo. This futuristic building was created by the architect I.M.
Pei, designer of the Pyramid of the Louvre. A few steps away is the
gigantic marble Citic Center, property of the provincial government
of Guangdong. In the port a giant panel bears the figures 999, the
logo of the San Jiu Enterprise Group, a pharmaceutical firm which
belongs to the People's Liberation Army.

Chinese businessmen are everywhere, absolutely everywhere.
And they are arrogant. Chinese money is flowing through those
neon tubes. Chinese companies own one-fifth of Hong Kong's total

business and a quarter of the cargos. They sell and distribute practically all of the food consumed by Hong Kong's 6.2 million residents each day. Guangdong Enterprises, a local branch of the provincial government, already supplies Hong Kong's markets with their fish and produce.

One estimate made in Beijing and published by the *Wall Street Journal* indicates that some 1,800 mainland Chinese businesses (including a thousand with Chinese government backing) are officially registered in the territory. About fifteen of these are listed on the stock exchange, and the total assets amount to at least $42.5 billion US. Some of these are state-owned companies. Others are run under the auspices of the central government or the provincial governments. Still others are affiliated with the Communist Party through the Communist Youth League or the People's Liberation Army.

Chinese investments grow each year by 25%. Three hundred mainland companies hope to join the ranks of the seventy companies listed on the Hong Kong stock exchange. They dream of one day becoming one of the thirty-three leading companies which make up the Hang Seng Index. The great majority of Chinese enterprises pour $65 billion US, or more than half of China's foreign reserves, into Hong Kong.

"This does not mean that this money will stay in Hong Kong," Richard Wang, a local financial analyst, points out. "It can leave the island. A certain amount goes to America, and some makes the round trip back to China."

Before June 1995, Beijing had invested $25 billion HK in the territory, or about 80% of its total foreign investments. Chinese companies control about 25% of Hong Kong's foreign trade, and own an impressive portfolio of commercial real estate, as well as 25% of Hong Kong's bank deposits in dollars, and 21% of its insurance policies.

The Hit Parade of Chinese Businesses in Hong Kong

China's strongest and most prominent financial presence in Hong Kong is, obviously, the Bank of China. It is one of only three banks authorized to print and issue dollars in Hong Kong, the other two being the London-based HSBC Holding PLC and Standard Chartered PLC.

The Bank of China is not listed on the exchange. It remains secretive about its activities, its clients, and their activities and profits. It is commonly known that the bank serves as the umbrella for eleven smaller banks and countless investment firms.

Number two among Chinese companies is the ubiquitous Citic Pacific, direct from the Beijing region. Over the past ten years it has grown considerably, and is now worth $10.3 billion US. This immense conglomerate, which operates in China and Hong Kong, owns a hodgepodge of real estate, shares in the telecommunications industry, airlines, credit unions, water treatment plants, and a steel mill. Since 1993, Citic Pacific has invested heavily in China, with profits earned in Hong Kong—$1.2 billion—in highways, bridges, and water distribution projects.

At its helm is Larry C. K. Yung, son of China's vice president, Rong Yiren. Yung crystallized the alliance of Chinese Communist power and hard-core capitalism. He is the Red Multimillionaire par excellence.

Citic Pacific is the very embodiment of the People's Republic of China transplanted to Hong Kong. When the Chinese government decided in April 1996 that the established British company Swire Pacific could no longer own a majority of shares of Hong Kong's airlines, Cathay Pacific and Dragon Air, it turned to Larry Yung. Citic Pacific, linked with the official China National Aviation Corporation, scooped up the shares. Its stake in Cathay Pacific rose from 10% to 25%; in Dragon Air, from 35% to 86%. Swire became a minority, with 43.9% of shares. A fabulous political deal disguised as a business deal.

(above) Skyscrapers are sprouting up like mushrooms. Soon, there will not be any room to walk between them.
(left) Emily Lau, lawmaker and former journalist. In 1984 she publicly rebuked Margaret Thatcher at a press conference.

(above) In 1995 there were 131,165 Filipinos employed as domestics in Hong Kong. *(right)* A billboard for a massage parlor hangs from a bamboo scaffolding. Most massage parlors are thinly disguised fronts for brothels.

紅太陽
Red Sun Beauty Massage

(above) Bar hostesses. They will dance with you or, for an "exit fee," spend the night with you.
(right) Queen's Road East. This has become a cliche of tourist guides. The Rolls Royces and Bentleys, some of them painted in voluptuous colors, are always visible.

(right) A cobbler in Wanchai. Wanchai and Mongkok are good destinations for those enamored of things Chinese. *(below)* The traditional bird promenade in Victoria Park.

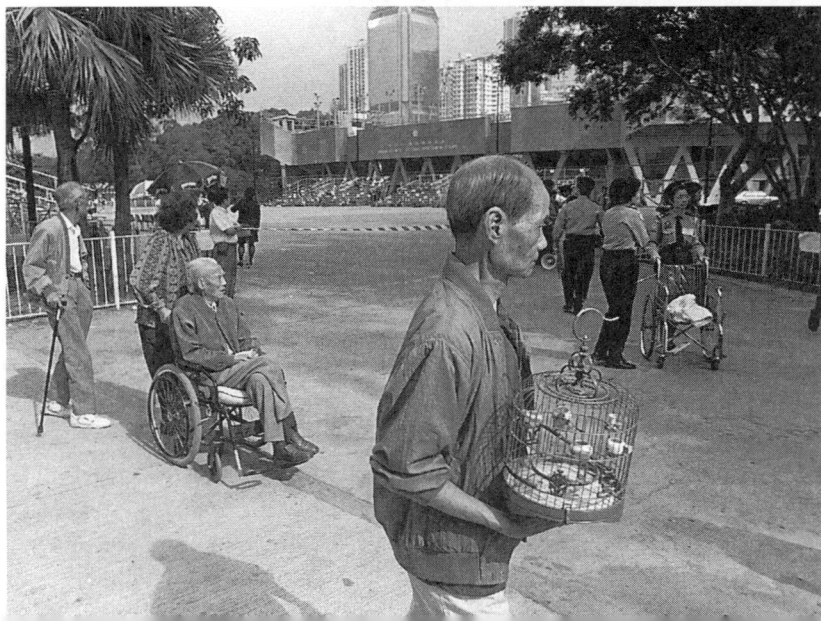

(*above*) Ducks in a restaurant window in Lan Kwai Fong.

(*left*) The Lan Kwai Fong quarter, a neighborhood of bars and restaurants where lonely expatriates gather.

(*right*) Two and a half million passengers ride the Hong Kong subways daily. Business takes place even on the trains. (*below*) The wharf for Kowloong-bound ferries. On the left, in the fog, the roof of Palace of Congress resembles a bird about to take flight. The Palace was the site of the handover ceremony on June 30, 1997.

(*above*) Pressure from the Communists in China on the local media has been rising. Even the celebrated English-language newspaper, the *South China Morning Post,* has tempered its content.

(*left*) Eight is a lucky number in Hong Kong. This billionaire's car is well protected.

The Bank of China, a spectacular steel and glass skyscraper, designed by I. M. Pei.

Soon Hong Kong Telecom, the local telephone company, will be next. 8% of its shares are owned by Citic. It will take 20% of the British firm Cable and Wireless, whose monopoly, projected until the year 2006, has been considerably depleted.

What of Larry Yung and his company? He is an indispensable contact for Western businessmen who want to invest in Hong Kong or China. This man can open all doors in Beijing for investors in China, where patience is essential for doing business.

A number of other Chinese businesses have also landed in Hong Kong. China Overseas Holding Ltd., founded in 1979, is headed by Sun Wenjie and has assets of several billion dollars. It belongs to the Chinese Ministry of Construction and is highly regarded by foreigners. Some of its most ambitious projects are proudly displayed in the top-floor reception area of its splendid headquarters—for example the terminal of the new futuristic Chek Lap Kok Airport, (which opened in July 1998, well behind schedule), and various opulent real-estate complexes.

But the skies have not always been sunny for China Overseas. After it opened its office in 1979 it struggled for survival until the early 1980s, hurt by falling real-estate prices and rising interest rates due to the uncertainty over the territory's future. Sun Wenjie is treasurer of the Hong Kong Chinese Enterprises Association, which, as its name suggests, works to introduce and develop businesses from mainland China.

The Shanghai Industrial Investment Company has the wind in its sails. It is based in Beijing, but most of its high-level directors come from the southern city of Shanghai. It specializes in import and export, real estate, finance, tourism, and the hotel industry. Other influential but more modest businesses include Beijing's Diaoyutai Guest House, where visiting Chinese heads of state are lodged; Triple International Ltd., an import-export company owned by the Planning Commission of the Chinese province of Hebei; and the China Youth Federation, which has real estate holdings.

All of these businesses, despite their low-key façades, handle millions of dollars in the territory.

The "Red Tycoons" and the Emperor's Sons

They are called "red tycoons" because, aside from their colossal fortunes, these men enjoy privileged contacts in the government of the People's Republic of China. For years, this has been indispensable to becoming rich in Hong Kong.

Larry C. K. Yung

Larry Yung, fifty-five years old, is an institution. A highly prized pawn of Beijing, he is known for his red Rolls Royce and his mansions in Hong Kong and Canada. Born into an important Shanghai family, he is a graduate of Stanford University in the United States. His role is eminently political. He is supported and guided by Beijing. He enjoys a flamboyant lifestyle as a member of Hong Kong's high society, race-horse owner, and Steward in the local Jockey Club, one of the twelve prestigious titles in this exclusive equestrian institution.

As president of Citic Pacific, Yung holds 18.5% of the shares of the company, which is controlled by the China International Trust and Investment Corporation of Beijing. The firm's profits grew from $333 million HK to $3.07 billion in 1995. Citic Pacific, directed by Larry Yung's father, China's vice president Rong Yiren, is in the forefront of China's investors in Hong Kong. Rong plays an essential role as the link between the family's business and the regime.

Larry Yung began his career in Hong Kong in 1978. With some of his cousins he founded Elcap, an electronics firm. The company grew, and he sold his shares to an American company. His resume shows that he later directed a software firm, which he also sold for a king's ransom to launch Citic.

Li Ka-shing

Sixty-eight-year-old Li Ka-shing is one of the richest men in the world. Originally from Guangdong Province, he is discreet, avoids reporters, and lives quietly in a gilded mansion in Hong Kong. Like all, or almost all the other magnates, this immigrant from the mainland started poor, selling artificial flowers. His fortune, made in the real estate business, is today estimated at $23 billion.

Closely tied to the Chinese authorities, he now holds capital in all sectors of the economy—real estate, telecommunications, energy, retail sales, and sporting goods. He is president, notably, of Cheung Kong and Hutchinson Whampoa.

In the first week of January 1997 he won an impressive roll of the dice, taking control of Hong Kong Electric, one of the two companies that supply electricity to the territory. His personal contacts with Beijing have garnered him a seat on the Preparatory Committee, which in December 1996 "elected" Hong Kong's chief of state, Tung Chee-hwa.

He also owns important real estate holdings in the People's Republic of China.

Yan Biao

Yan Biao is one of Beijing's most loyal lieutenants, and the head of China Resources Ltd. He deals in beer, real estate, and refrigerators.

"We want to make a *hong* [large commercial company] out of this business," declares the thirty-four-year-old tycoon.

The best-known *hongs* are Jardine Matheson Holdings Ltd., named after two of the world's biggest drug traffickers (see Introduction, p. 14), Swire Pacific, and Hutchinson Whampoa Ltd., which is now controlled by the billionaire Li Ka-shing.

Yan Biao has all the right stuff. He prepared himself well, earning a business degree from the University of Chicago. But above all, he is controlled by the Chinese. He is an "emperor," as the mainlanders sent to Hong Kong by Chinese businesses call themselves. In ten years of work in the territory, he played a role in the building of China Resources, the commercial branch of the Chinese Ministry of Commerce and Economic Cooperation. He favors well-tailored suits, is fluent in Cantonese, and speaks like a tycoon, peppering his sentences with expressions like "strategic investments" and "retail concepts."

From 1992 to 1995, China Resources nearly tripled its profits, from $100 million HK to $285 million.

"We have an advantage," he explained to the *Wall Street Journal*, his favorite newspaper. "We understand China, but we use Western administration methods. We are not the slaves of that bureaucracy, which has stunted the growth of many other Chinese businesses."

Charles Yeung

This head of Glorious Sun Enterprises, a jeans manufacturer, has always navigated between two worlds—the People's Republic of China, where he was born and raised, and Hong Kong.

"I am an excellent bridge," he explains. "I know the culture and values of China, but I also know how things work in Hong Kong." This is the success secret for a number of businessmen of his generation.

The baby-faced, forty-one-year-old Yeung is the archetype of those who will play a major role in the Hong Kong of tomorrow. He knows how to make money, and at the same time he enjoys the confidence of officials across the border.

Mr. Yeung left Guangdong, his native province, at the age of nineteen for Hong Kong, where he started out earning six dollars a day as a delivery boy for a garment company. Four years later, he and a few of his friends pooled their savings, $200,000 HK, and created their own jeans factory, the ancestor of Glorious Sun. They flooded the local market, as well as Australia and China. Very soon they were making clothing for well-known American brands such as the Gap.

Before the historic year of 1997, his company was listed on the exchange, and its value is climbing. Yeung is nursing even grander ambitions. He plans to create a jeans empire before the year 2000, with the opening of one hundred stores in as many cities, mostly in China.

The Sons of Chinese Archbishops: Mr. Leung and Mr. Fok

They call them the "red princelings"—the sixty sons and daughters of men close to the Chinese regime since the 1950s, who sit in the new Legislative Chamber. From princes of finance, they have gone on to become influential politicians, thanks to their role in the Parliament, designated by Beijing to replace LEGCO, which was elected under the British system. They are "red" not by ideology, but through their parents' contacts. Money motivates them, not politics.

One of the most important is Leung Chun-ying, forty-three years old. His father was a police officer with im-portant contacts in the seat of Beijing's government. The ever-smiling Mr. Leung directs an impressive real-estate agency, C. Y. Leung & Co., which has developed into a colossus thanks to deals made throughout the world in 1995. It now owns branches in 170 cities, in 32 countries.

Leung Chun-ying won his highest post in China when Beijing nominated him vice president of the Preparatory Committee. By his side are some of the figures most loyal to Beijing: the Chinese Minister of Foreign Affairs Qian Qichen, Henry Fok, and Zhou Nan, the Hong Kong-based director of the quite-official New China Agency—not to mention Tung Chee-hwa, the chief of state. Barring a change in the Communist leadership, and if Leung retains his aura of sanctity, he will no doubt be the successor to Tung. This policeman's son-cum-senator could well be president.

Timothy Fok Tsun-ting is generally considered the "prince among princes" in the camp of those who favor mainland China. He is the eldest son of the most influential businessman in Hong Kong, the multimillionaire Henry Fok Ying-tung—the very same man who bailed out Tung Chee-hwa when his Orient Overseas was on the brink of failure in the 1980s. This obviously created close ties. The young Timothy, after finishing his studies in the United States, always accompanied his father on visits to government friends in Beijing. He once even sat on Jiang Zemin's lap.

He wants to represent the generation of technocrat tycoons. "Our chance," he says, "is to get hooked up with China."

Will Chinese Businesses Get Special Treatment?

Before the handover, when the British were still in charge, they monitored businesses, ever vigilant for violations of the laws on competition. The Independent Commission Against Corruption (ICAC) was created in 1977, directly under the aegis of the governor's office. The ICAC was a success from the very start. In 1995, according to official statistics, it received 3,232 reports of corruption, including 1,878 in the private sector.

Today, with the British gone, the Chinese will be free to let their imagination take flight. Shady deals could proliferate. In addition, foreign investors and businessmen fear that Chinese businesses will automatically be given special treatment in the distribution of markets. If this is the case, Hong Kong's reputation will be tarnished. The island would also lose its principal advantages—its openness and its competition-friendly laws.

"We must not allow Chinese businesses to go above the law," affirms Stuart Leckie, president of Fidelity Investment Management. Of course not. But what can be done to prevent it?

Even before the handover, the stock exchange granted more favorable treatment to mainland companies over Hong Kong's. In 1993, aiming to become the Chinese Wall Street, it gave them extra incentives.

If this trend is to increase, if the exchange lets go of the standards that made Hong Kong's market one of the most open and attractive in the world, foreign investors could well head for other financial centers.

A FRENCHMAN'S SUCCESS

Among Hong Kong's magnates there is one who is quite extraordinary. He has French nationality and is among the 4,500 people who frequent Hong Kong's French consulate.

You notice him every year, between two glasses of champagne and three petits fours, at the Bastille Day celebration organized by the French authorities in the territory.

Our seventy-two-year-old "Frenchman" stands out from the crowd. Flaunting a diamond-studded Swiss wristwatch, he speaks not a single word of French, can hardly make himself understood in English, mangles his Mandarin, and massacres Cantonese, his native tongue. A model self-made man.

This odd duck, this rarest of Frenchmen, is Mr. Cheng Yu-tung, a Hong Kong multimillionaire with strong ties to the Communist Chinese regime. He is probably one of the richest Frenchmen in the world, with a family fortune estimated at $52 billion.

Cheng obtained his French passport in 1991 as an insurance policy, in case his situation in Hong Kong ever turns sour and he needs to escape. At first glance, however, he has nothing at all to fear from Beijing.

The day after the student demonstration in Tienanmen Square was crushed in 1989, many corporate leaders considered boycotting the People's Republic of China until things cooled down. Not Cheng—he invested even more. When the central city of Wuhan needed money to finance a new bridge over China's longest river, the Yangtze, Cheng's New World Group came to the rescue. When Guangdong needed a new tollway, this same group took on the project. Far from upsetting Cheng, Tienanmen Square made him rich.

He has plenty of other strong cards in his hand. He grew up with the mayor of Canton, Li Ziliu. He knows China's president, Jiang Zemin, personally, as well as many other officials. It is not surprising that he became one of the principal investors in the People's Republic of China.

However, none of these accomplishments explain his bizarre diplomatic feat of obtaining a passport from the French consulate in Hong Kong. In this troubled age of taboos on immigration, when France is so stingy in granting nationality, one can only wonder how he did it.

The answer is simple. Cheng "contributed" considerably to the promotion of French culture in Hong Kong. He generously opened his wallet to finance various artistic activities, including "French May," an annual festival held by the French consulate. The consular officers expressed their deep gratitude to this patron of the arts by "kindly" issuing him a passport. As a further show of thanks, in case the passport was not enough, he was named Chevalier of Arts and Letters in September 1996 by M. Douste Blazy, then French Minister of Culture, during his first visit to his adopted country.

His eldest son, Henry, who at age fifty handles his aging father's affairs, has also benefited from the largesse of the French consuls: he became a Frenchman as well. He is president of the Better Hong Kong Foundation, a lobby group founded by twenty tycoons, including the Cheng family. The foundation promotes Hong Kong with the motto: "Investors have nothing to fear! The arrival of the Chinese will not change a thing!" The year before the handover, the foundation invited hundreds of foreign journalists, and put them up, gratis, in the most luxurious hotels. The idea was to re-establish Hong Kong's image in the Western media after it was tarnished by a lengthy *Fortune* article entitled "The Death of Hong Kong" (June 26, 1995).

Rolls Royce Number 8888

Who is this mysterious Cheng, dubbed "Doctor" by his colleagues? Unassuming in appearance, he wears the traditional gray three-piece suit of Hong Kong nabobs, with various matching ties and silk pocket handkerchiefs. His main office, on the thirty-second floor of the New World Tower on Queen's Road, in the very heart of Central, dominates the bay. There he displays all his trophies, diplomas, and cups, accumulated around the world over the course of his career.

Cheng lives on Repulse Bay, with a view of the South China Sea. He gets around town in a Rolls Royce with the license plate number 8888, a rare plate that cost him $150,000 at an auction twenty-two years ago. "I know people who would spend fortunes to buy it from me," he says bemusedly. The number eight symbolizes fortune in China. Four eights—one can only imagine . . . .

Cheng was born in 1925 in Shun Tak, a village in the southern province of Guangdong. He emigrated in the 1960s to Macao and then to Hong Kong with $200 in his pocket, so he claims. He went to work for a jewelry store in Kowloon, kept his nose to the grindstone, and eventually bought the business. Today he presides, almost single-handedly, over a network of the colony's richest businesses: the New World Development Co. Ltd., New World Hotels Ltd., and Chow Tai Fook Enterprises. He also co-owns, with Lyonnaise des Eaux, the rights to distribute water to Macao until the year 2000.

In the early 1980s, Cheng won an incredible game of poker. He accepted the project for the construction of the superb futuris-tic Hong Kong Convention and Exhibition Center, the Palace of Congresses that no one wanted because of the uncertainty hanging over Hong Kong's future. It was here that the formal handover ceremony took place on June 30, 1997, in a wing of the glass-and-steel main building, whose undulating roof evokes the image of a bird taking flight. Right in front is the New World Hotel—which also belongs to Cheng.

"I like to do what I think I should do, rather than follow the crowd," he says. A good number of his successes are due to the gambler in him.

Cheng is director of the Hang Seng Bank Ltd., a member of the Hong Kong and Shanghai Banking Corp. Ltd., and head of many other companies whose stocks are traded on the Hong Kong Stock Exchange. His hotel operations have been listed on the New York Stock Exchange since September 1995. Through the Renaissance chain, this "Frenchman" owns 144 hotels, with a total of 46,000 rooms, in the Asian Pacific region, Europe, and North America. In mainland China his group invested $25 billion HK in 6 years. He owns highways, toll bridges, electric plants, theme parks, and more.

The Cheng family also heads the biggest chain of jewelry stores in Hong Kong and Macao: Chow Tai Fook Jewelry Company, Ltd. His relatives have holdings in real estate, petroleum, and gas in the United States as well.

At the same time that he deals in these quite diverse business activities, Mr. Cheng keeps a vigilant eye on his image. As he has done with France, he finances various cultural projects and charities in Hong Kong as well as abroad.

As a result of his contributions, aside from his French passport, he has received numerous titles and decorations around the world, in Macao, Toronto, Beijing, and Malaysia, where the Sultan of Selangor personally honored him.

In 1993 the *South China Morning Post*, a local English-language daily, voted him Businessman of the Year.

It is a pity that "Monsieur Cheng" does not speak a word of French. Perhaps when he retires he will find the time to learn, in one of his many homes.

FREEDOM OF RELIGION

A Refuge for Catholic Priests

March 1997. Number Four Robinson Road in the middle-class neighborhood of Mid Levels resembles a housing project with wide green picture windows.

A sign at the front entrance reads "Bishop Lei International House." It is a middle-budget hotel with two hundred-fifty rooms, a guest house of sorts, but a very special one. It was rebuilt in 1996 by high-ranking Catholic officials to house one hundred-fifty Chinese priests of the diocese, should they ever be turned out into the street.

The building, situated in the middle of a confused web of concrete bridges overlooking a lush forest, was blessed by Cardinal Wu, as a black-marble commemorative plaque points out. For the moment it still functions an a hotel.

Similarly, the Baptist church Che Fu, founded in 1988 by the Reverend John Ho and an American missionary from Georgia, Donna Kirby, is considering the eventual transformation of its prayer stalls into a shelter.

Religious leaders do not fear for their lives, but—knowing the Chinese Communist regime—they are afraid that in a few years they will no longer be able to exert their authority as they have in the past. The question haunting churches, temples, and pagodas is: Will the Chinese officials be able to respect our religious diversity?

"Double" Catholicism in China

As Father Vincent-Paul Toccoli, tireless spokesman for the French Catholic community, points out, "The Chinese will probably adapt freedom of religion to their norms by deciding to regulate it." Therein lies the problem. In religion, as in so many other fields, notably politics, the Chinese Communists will no doubt insist on regulating everything. To complicate matters, in their eyes, anything remotely connected with religion is immediately suspect, as is any organization or group of individuals which refuses to pledge its allegiance to the regime.

"All you have to do is take a look at what's going on in mainland China, where freedom of religion is provided for in the Constitution," remarks Father Toccoli.

In fact, one need not even cite the extreme case of Tibet, where the Buddhism of the Dalai Lama is strictly forbidden, and his followers are sought out and punished. The unusual way in which the Catholic hierarchy functions in the People's Republic of China is sadly revealing. In fact, two "Catholic" churches exist—one which answers to Rome, one which does not.

The latter, with the significant name "Chinese Patriotic Catholic Association," is the only one authorized to exist since the break between the Vatican and Beijing in 1957. This "patriotic" association, unrecognized by the Pope, has four million members, a thousand priests, and fifty-five bishops, who are nominated under Beijing's authority. As an official organization, it has the right to call meetings and to give mass—in short, the right to exist and proselytize. It is controlled by the regime. This is the "official" Catholic Church, which has sworn allegiance to the Communist Party and preaches a non-reformist Christianity not in accord with the guidelines of Vatican II.

Behind the Wall, however, there is also an "underground" church that survives, called the Church of Silence. It is clandestine and loyal to Rome. Its clergy work on the grass-roots level, in direct contact with the population.

Today, non-official ties have been established one by one between the religious communities supported by the Chinese regime and the communities that are more or less underground and unrecognized. It has been frequently whispered that the Vatican and Beijing could become reconciled someday; what is more, this is one of Pope

John Paul II's most cherished wishes. In 1989, in Seoul, he expressed for the first time his desire to visit China. But Beijing has a condition for the re-establishment of relations with the Vatican: Rome must break with Taiwan.

For the moment, the breach is being filled bit by bit, but still remains.

Some observers do not exclude the possibility that the Chinese might create a branch of the Patriotic Catholic Association in Hong Kong, which would result in a competition between two separate Catholic churches, as it has in China.

It appears the Pope has found a way to avoid this. On October 20, 1996, he appointed two new bishops to Hong Kong. They have distinct personalities and are perceived differently by Beijing. This was certainly no accident.

The first is a theologian, Father Joseph Zen. Born in 1932, he speaks several languages, including Cantonese and the Shanghai dialect and, most important, spends six months of each year working with seminaries in Shanghai, Wuhan, Xian, Shijiazhuang, Beijing, and Shenyang. He operates under the ubiquitous authority of the Patriotic Catholic Association.

Zen has been a teacher to several young Chinese clergy with close ties to the regime. In the worst scenario, if relations between the regime and the Vatican should turn ugly, they would no doubt listen to him.

At the same time, the Pope appointed Father Joseph Tung, who was born in Hong Kong in 1939. The Chinese authorities are more suspicious of Tung. With his twin appointment of bishops, the Pope showed himself to be a shrewd politician in his own right.

The Churches As They Stand Now
In the period preceding the Communist Chinese arrival in Hong

Kong, the Catholic hierarchy had two bishops who complement each other, one more or less accepted by Beijing because of his collaboration with the Patriotic Association, the other regarded with more suspicion.

At the top of the hierarchy, these two new bishops must answer to the real "boss" of Hong Kong's Catholics, Cardinal John B. Wu Cheng-chung. He is the highest-ranking official in a diocese that counts seventy Chinese priests and one American.

A census conducted by the Church of Hong Kong in August 1996 found that Hong Kong had a total of 242,391 Catholics, divided as follows:

84,954 on the island of Hong Kong proper (35%)
102,933 in Kowloon (43%)
54,504 in the New Territories (22%)

These figures do not take into account Hong Kong's tens of thousands of Filipinos, the territory's most significant foreign minority, a large number of whom practice the Catholic religion. Numbering about 500,000, Catholics account for about half of Hong Kong's Christians, or less than 1/10 of a population of 6 million, 98% of which is Chinese. The rest of the territory's Christians consists of Protestants, who first arrived in 1841. Among them, Baptists are the most numerous, followed by Lutherans, Seventh-Day Adven-tists, Anglicans, the Church of Christ of China, Methodists, and Pentacostalists.

However, the main religions of Hong Kong remain Buddhism and Taoism.

The most famous of the territory's 350 temples is that of Wong Tai Sin, built at the beginning of the century. It is the local version of Lourdes. Believers approach an image of the Great Sage, who created the elixir of immortality at the age of fifteen. They come to seek cures from illness (as well as the occasional horse tip).

Other religions include Islam, Hinduism, Confucianism, and Animism. There are also countless pantheistic sects, who view nature as divine and represent their gods as monkeys, the sea, the earth, or the embodiment of justice. In Hong Kong, religions and superstitions frequently overlap.

A "Rosary" of Questions: What Will Become of the Schools?

The handover could have the sharpest, most brutal, and most immediate repercussions for the schools run by the churches. The religious communities, along with the communications industry, are eagerly awaiting Beijing's reactions and decisions. Although the Protestants and Catholics account for only 8% of the population, they administer 40% of the territory's primary and secondary schools.

The Catholic Church administers 329 schools, with a total of 280,149 pupils. The Protestant community, with 1,200 congregations and 260,000 members, has three universities: Chung Chi College at the University of Hong Kong, Hong Kong Baptist University, and Lignan College. Protestants also administer 121 secondary schools and, notably, 233 kindergartens.

How are the Chinese going to deal with this culturally diverse situation? Would they—could they—allow hundreds of schools to float freely in a bubble of nonallegiance? That would be totally contrary to what has occurred on the mainland. The slogan "One country, two systems" could well be subject to serious distortions.

One hundred days before the handover, in March 1997, China's Ministry of Foreign Affairs, Qian Qichen, announced his intention to rewrite outmoded school textbooks. An Englishman and a Chinese would most likely treat the Opium Wars quite differently.

Not surprisingly, textbooks from the British period which do not mention the Sino-British Joint Declaration of 1984 or the Chinese Parliament's Basic Law of 1990 will be revised. But there is the risk that other issues, less directly linked with Hong Kong's history and more ideological in nature, will appear in the new textbooks. As all totalitarian countries know, indoctrination begins at school!

What About the Hospitals?

Hospitals, which are certainly not political, are crucial for the territory. The religious presence in them is considerable. The Catholic Church, through Caritas, administers six hospitals (with a total of 3,030 beds), fourteen clinics, and seventeen maternity hospitals, as well as retirement homes and student residences.

The Protestants administer seven hospitals (with a total of 3,463 beds), twenty-four clinics, sixty-one charity wards, twenty-nine rest homes, three schools for the hard of hearing, and twenty-one centers for the handicapped—as well as five international hotels.

What will become of this empire? Will not the Communists want to impose their usual bureaucracy and reorganize a system that functions perfectly well? This is to be feared, say optimists. It is a certainty, say pessimists.

The very organization and autonomy of the churches are now in question. Will Beijing allow the various churches to stay in their present locations? Will the Catholic Cathedral, located at One Kent Road, still be able to occupy its several buildings, including the parish house? What relations will the church officials be able to maintain with the outside world? Will the Catholics be able to work in constant contact with Rome? Will their publications be controlled? How will mail from Rome be delivered? How will the respective churches' subsidies be administered? Will the clergy, in particular the one hundred fifty Catholic priests, be allowed to hold passports?

In January 1995 the Mission of Churches of Hong Kong, a Protestant organization, published a document in seven parts and signed by seven hundred ministers, titled *Regarding the Special Administrative Region*.

Article 5 reads: "We wish to continue to serve the society of Hong Kong by offering a quality education, as well as social and medical services."

In Article 6 the Mission affirms: "The goal is to allow the citizens of Hong Kong to enjoy the benefits of democracy and human rights. The churches should be able to continue to enjoy freedom of religion, as well as the freedom to communicate and cooperate with other regions. The churches of Hong Kong must not only be able to develop locally, they must also be able to play a unique role with the Churches of China as well as in the whole world."

Not all Protestants, however, have adopted the same position. Of their own accord, forty-seven church officials, ministers, and theologians proposed in late 1996 to participate in the October celebration of the anniversary of the creation of the People's Republic of China. The idea made waves in the Protestant community, but it was finally rejected. However, this initiative indicates that there will be no lack of collaborators—Protestant or otherwise—eager to win the favor of the new masters.

Since 1995 other clergymen, especially the young, have decided to leave.

"Many young people have had enough and have left," notes Kim Kwong Chan, chaplain of Chung Chi College at the University of Hong Kong. The same is true of the colleagues of Li Cho Yiu. When he graduated from the Hong Kong Theological School in 1990, there were eighteen students in his class. Today, half of them work in Chinese churches in San Francisco, Toronto, and Sydney.

However, the vast majority of Hong Kong's clergy intend to stay in the territory as long as they can.

Traditions: Buddhism and *Feng Shui*
There are also traditions that overlap with religions. The Chinese of Beijing will be more comfortable dealing with them than

with organized religions. Unlike Western religions, superstitions do not function as "foreign agents of penetration," an oft-repeated Beijing expression.

The Chinese are not afraid of these customs, which mark the life of the former British colony. They are Chinese; they will deal with them by adapting them, if necessary.

Traditions are everywhere in Hong Kong. It is impossible to take one step without encountering one.

Offerings are traditionally made before an image of Buddha, surrounded by a few burning sticks of incense. You can see this at construction sites and in front of all businesses, even prostitution bars and massage parlors. This practice is as much a part of daily life as eating or drinking.

A popular story on the island illustrates the inhabitants' devotion. In the 1960s the prestigious and exclusive Jockey Club had a streak of bad luck, including the death of a jockey. To exorcise the bad luck and end the string of mishaps, a neo-Buddhist ceremony was organized over the course of four days and three nights on the lawn of the Happy Valley Racetrack, in the presence of sixty-eight monks and forty-eight nuns, with forty thousand people in attendance.

The Chinese of Hong Kong, like those of the mainland, have a profound belief in geomancy, or *feng shui*, which literally means "wind" and "water." Is it a philosophy, an art, a science, or a superstition? The essence of *feng shui* is the harmony between man and nature.

Feng shui masters are highly revered and are among the highest-paid people in the territory. Some masters require an appointment several years in advance. When you construct a building or decide to move, you consult one of these masters. After studying the "force of the elements" (water, wind, sky, earth, rivers), he decides whether or not the selected site or the apartment is propitious. Legend has it that if you heed his advice, good luck and prosperity are assured. If not. . . .

Everyone, from the grocer to the insurance agent, respects his expertise. One well-known Hong Kong bank regularly sends its clients a *feng shui* index revealing the investment advice of a master compared with that of its own analysts. Not surprisingly, they roughly coincide. This is an original and astute advertising concept, for people in Hong Kong follow the advice of *feng shui* specialists unquestioningly.

Over the course of centuries there are examples of entire villages being abandoned because the local feng shui was upset by a disruption of the cosmic balance. When the first subway tunnels were being dug, Hong Kong had to call upon European miners—the Chinese did not want to risk disturbing the spirits of the earth.

In 1980, the peasants of the island of Lantau struck it rich thanks to *feng shui*. They sued the maritime authorities for the sudden death of their chickens after a *feng shui* violation by a boat anchored near their lands.

During the construction of a high-rise apartment building on a cliff, a *feng shui* specialist expressed his concern that the building would prevent the dragon living on a nearby hill from contemplating the sea by blocking his view. The master's observation was immediately heeded. The terrified architects decided to pierce a hole in the building sufficiently large for the dragon to contemplate the sea. The realtors and owners of the lost apartments were out of luck.

The way in which deceased relatives are buried is likewise of vital importance. If the tomb does not face in the direction of the sea, as recommended by *feng shui*, future generations of the family will be punished. Bad luck will plague them for centuries.

Numbers also have special significance. The number four is forbidden because the word for "four" is homonymous with the word for "death." Therefore, one must not live on the fourth floor of a building, or on the fourteenth, etc. However, the twenty-eighth floor is highly recommended: twenty represents prosperity, and eight fortune.

Colors also have specific meanings. Red is always highly recommended. In this Chinese environment where money is worshipped, it represents good luck.

And it is forbidden to place a bed facing the entrance to the bedroom—this is how the dead are laid out!

The Clans

Some of the customs of clans date back to 1664, during the Qing Dynasty, when 6,000 clans were formed. They were given hereditary ownership of immense areas of land in the New Territories.

Upon the arrival of the British, these clans obtained leases on their property for a period of 999 years. Today, their descendants still administer these lands. For example, part of the fishing village of Shek O, on the southeastern part of the island, belongs to a handful of families. Thirteen generations of the Li clan have lived there for two centuries. The family's matriarch, Li Lau Ping Tai, was born eighty-one years ago in Shek O. This still hearty woman enjoys pointing out the tombs behind her home, which date back to the nineteenth century.

Many members of these clans have become immensely rich by renting out their lands and developing them from generation to generation. For example, the Tang family owns 60% of Wang Toi Shan, thanks to a custom whereby each male has erected one new building in the village in his lifetime. This has allowed the Tangs and many other families to build regularly, extend their holdings, and maintain their influence on the village.

A stone's throw from the futuristic skyscrapers of the Central, these clans still live in an earlier century, in the middle of the countryside, observing sometimes brutal traditions.

For example, they scoff at the idea of educating their daughters. "What for?" they say. "When they grow up, they'll just go off and allow another clan to multiply—maybe a rival clan." Instead, they simply feed and raise their daughters until they are ready to leave home. "That's already not such a bad deal," murmurs Feng.

Thanks to their sometimes enormous inheritances, clan members rarely work. The men spend their time playing *mahjong*, the favorite pastime in Hong Kong, at least among the older inhabitants. Just walk along the little streets of Wanchai or Causeway Bay. The *mahjong* establishments are easy to find because of the special clicking sound—the sound of dominos striking the tables.

FREEDOM OF THE PRESS

Shortly before the handover, freedom of the press was still the rule. The English, to be sure, gave Hong Kong democracy quite late, but still one must recognize that newspapers of all types have the freedom to write what they want, on any subject, with the exception of hard-core pornography. For Asia this is extremely unusual, almost unique, and sufficiently important to deserve special mention.

What will happen now that the British, who once ensured this plurality, are gone? Obviously, the subject of freedom of the press is far more uncertain than any other. No one can say for sure how things will evolve, although it is to be feared that China will silence titles, voices and images. Hong Kong's press certainly will be less subject to the government's power than Beijing's. But it may gradually lose that proud independence which has made its reputation, many experts agree. Even before Chinese party officials arrived in Hong Kong, disturbing signals were already coming from Beijing.

Bad Omens

It is hard to say why the Chinese would allow Hong Kong's press to criticize them at all, when they have strictly forbidden this on the mainland since 1949. The journalists of the People's Republic of

China are militants loyal to the regime. In the land of Mao, "journalism" rhymes with "submission." This is a *sine qua non* condition.Every day, Chinese editors recite an oath of allegiance to the state, especially on the occasion of important events which could endanger its stability—for example, the death of Deng Xiaoping on February 20, 1997.

That morning, the daily newspapers of the capital all published the exact same black-and-white photograph of the patriarch and identical commentaries in the form of eulogies. The order had come loud and clear from above, dictated by the State Party via the Department of Propaganda, directed by Ding Guangen.

The Chinese press' state of total decay and poverty—intellectual as well as technical—is what Westerners find most striking. How can one believe in the credibility of this State—a permanent member of the United Nations Security Council—when one reads its terrible press? Impossible!

The *New York Times* featured a revealing comment by Wu Guogua, formerly editor-in-chief of the *People's Daily* and currently professor at the University of Hong Kong. He considers the greatest accomplishment of the Chinese press in the past ten years to be the publication of international news items, formerly a taboo. The only time the millstone was taken off the neck of the press was during the three weeks preceding the Tiananmen Square uprising, when newspapers were able to adopt an unprecedented candor due to the general panic at the highest levels of the government.

Certain reporters openly defied the authorities by attempting to show that the country was functioning normally, and that it was not going through a period of insurrection. In short, they claimed that this was not a return to the Cultural Revolution, as the party officials had unanimously proclaimed. This was a crime of *lèse majesté* committed by courageous journalists, one for which they paid later.

The Case of Jimmy Lai

In the future, how will Chinese officials, accustomed as they are to a docile press, react to the sophistication and diversity of tone in the Hong Kong press?

There is little point for Beijing to assure anyone of their fifty-year obligation to respect laws in effect in the territory, in particular freedom of the press, which is guaranteed by Article 27 of the Basic Law. No one would believe it, because even the Chinese Constitution protects these liberties.

As Michel Bonin, director of the French Center of Studies on Contemporary China, points out:

> The only victim singled out by Chinese terrorists in the colony was an announcer burned alive in his car in 1967 because he ridiculed the Chinese government in his broadcasts. Without going to these extremes, the government of Deng Xiaoping also did everything in its power to impede the survival of magazines such as *Zhenming* and *Jiushi niandai*, which made the mistake of exposing corruption and power struggles in the Chinese ruling class.

Especially revealing is the case of Jimmy Lai, which shows the Communists' deeply-rooted refusal to tolerate the slightest bit of mischief from the press.

Sporting a crewcut which gives him a false resemblance to Tung Chee-hwa, Jimmy Lai is one of the thousands of refugees who fled mainland China in the 1960s.

Like many others who made their fortune in Hong Kong, he arrived via Macao at the age of twelve, with a one-way ticket and a handful of dollars. He was a billionaire within a few years. He made his fortune in textiles, as many others have.

In *Remembers*, an interesting collection of personal reminiscences published in 1996 by Sally Blyth and Ian Wotherspoon, he reflects on his incredible rise: "I became a foreman at twenty. In the early 1980s I had the biggest casual-wear factory in Hong Kong. In 1981, I launched my own business, Giordano."

In Asia, Giordano is a poor man's version of France's Cacharel, or Ralph Lauren in the United States. It is a label of low-priced jeans and sports shirts for young people. The Giordano name on the label helped to ensure its success.

In 1989, during the Tienanmen Square events, Jimmy Lai immediately sided with the students because he "admired their courage."

"It was a revealing experience, as if China were my mother and I had never been able to speak to her before!" He printed T-shirts for the students in his factories and then, drawn toward politics and newspapers, this self-made man entered the world of the press. No doubt he felt a need to become known outside of the world of commerce.

In 1990, he founded the popular weekly *Next*, and in 1995, the daily *Apple Daily*.

"The intense work of the media during Tienanmen made me understand the importance of the press," he explains.

His two publications, often sensationalist and always critical of the Chinese system, enjoy a wide circulation and have earned an enviable place in the Hong Kong press.

Next, with a circulation of 250,000 in 1997, is by far the widest-read magazine in Hong Kong. People would fight to get a copy of *Next* in southern China, a situation which obviously intensified Beijing's ire toward Jimmy Lai.

Next is crammed with scandalous articles, photos of nude women, and—worst of all—violent attacks on Communist corruption and other practices. Its principle targets are Hong Kong personalities who have sided with Beijing.

"In spite of its gossip, *Next* is respected for having had the courage to take a stand," says Jimmy Lai. "We have attacked China a great deal, but I've never regretted what we have published. It reflects my own feelings!"

He ended up paying dearly for such diatribes against China.

"Two years after opening our Giordano boutiques in China," he recounts, "I had to sell the majority of my shares in the business because the Chinese authorities were harassing my businesses on the mainland and intimidating my employees. It was a little after the controversial article I published on [former prime minister] Li Peng."

This article, or polemic, which Jimmy Lai wrote in 1990, made the Beijing officials lose what little patience they had left. To be sure, Jimmy Lai had not minced words. He accused Li Peng of having directly caused the repression of Tienanmen, calling him a "son of a turtle egg" (a Chinese euphemism for "bastard") and expressed the wish that he would "drop dead in the street."

Not surprisingly, the reaction of the Chinese Communists was immediate and severe. Jimmy Lai had to divest himself of Giordano just when it was expanding in Asia. Reporters from *Next* and *Apple Daily* were denied entry visas to China.

The worst was yet to come.

In late February 1997, after numerous repercussions, everything was finally ready for the listing on the stock exchange of the Next Media Group (the press group that published the weekly *Next*), which had been purchased a year earlier by a powerful Chinese firm, the bank Sun Hung Kai International. Although the exchange had given the green light for the listing, however, the Chinese group picked up its marbles—and its dollars—and pulled out with no explanation. Peter Fung, director of Sun Hung Kai, followed Beijing's order to the letter—amounting to a death sentence for *Next*. The Chinese Communists could not tolerate the thought of such a rebellious publication winning its stock-exchange stripes in a region that was about to become part of the People's Republic of China.

Before Sun Hung Kai, twelve backers of *Next* had pulled out in the course of three years, including Smith New Court Far East Ltd., which was bought out by the American firm of Merrill Lynch.

In fear for his life, Jimmy Lai may have to flee Chinese persecution abroad, probably to North America. One need not pity him, however, as he has a nest egg of $100 million in the United States.

"Information," he says, "is not the key to Hong Kong's future success. The main thing will be to keep the existing structure that defends law and order in place, and to maintain the market economy."

Beijing's Weapons: Publicity and Money

During the course of 1997, as the day of the handover approached, the Communists brought more pressure to bear on the press. Financial constraints grew tighter and *Next* was not the only publication to feel the squeeze.

Pro-Chinese advertisers pulled their ads one by one from newspapers considered too critical of Beijing in favor of those more obedient to their "master's voice." Blacklists of publications not sanctioned by Beijing were secretly circulated in Hong Kong's financial circles. It was forbidden to invest a single dollar in a blacklisted publication. Little by little, the Communist Chinese won through intimidation. The publications understood that if they wanted to survive they would have to concede to Beijing.

With a few courageous exceptions, most of the media softened the tone of their editorials, and criticism of Beijing became less frequent. Hong Kong's press put on rose-colored glasses. Even the famous English-language daily, the *South China Morning Post,* watered down its commentaries. Self-censorship went into effect.

Similar developments occured on radio stations controlled by RTHK. Though there were some fearless programs, including Tai Keen Man's morning talk show, many radio writers bit their tongues, well aware that after July 1 the entire annual budget of RTHK—$57.7 million US of public money—would be voted by the new Parliament loyal to Beijing.

Finally, it is instructive to recount the story of Star TV.

In 1991, Rupert Murdoch had just gained control of this satellite station, which broadcasts through a number of channels across Asia, featuring sports, American series, and soap operas. Star TV also offered among its diverse programs the new and highly promising BBC Television. It did not last.

After a few weeks, Star TV had to give up BBC for good, as well as international news, on the orders of the Chinese, who were furious over a documentary on Mao which they deemed "irreverent." Star TV was richly rewarded for giving up BBC Television. It is now ubiquitous in the hotels of China.

An Imposing Diversity of Titles

Over the years, Hong Kong has fostered an imposing media empire. Various major international news agencies like Reuters and Agence France- Presse have regional offices there. It is the home of the Asian edition of the *International Herald Tribune*, Dow Jones's *Asian Wall Street Journal* and its protégé, the well-known weekly *Far Eastern Economic Review*, founded in 1946, with a current circulation of 65,000. The latter's main competitor, *Asiaweek* (circulation, 20,000), published by Time Warner, is also based in Hong Kong.

Will they stay? Will they leave?

Among the foreign media present on the island, the huge British agency Reuters was the first to close up shop and relocate its regional office in Singapore. The major American newspapers, such as the *Wall*

Street Journal, are ready to leave upon the first snag they encounter. Many alternate cities are under consideration, including Manila.

Among English-language publications, the best known daily is unquestionably the *South China Morning Post* (circulation, 115,000). Founded in 1903 and owned at one time by Rupert Murdoch, it was sold in 1993 to Robert Kuok, a wealthy Chinese-Malaysian businessman who is an advisor to Beijing and president of Kerry Media.

Kerry Media already owns a third of shares in Hong Kong's station TVB. So far, the *South China Morning Post* has traditionally been favorably disposed toward the British colonists. But times are changing. The paper's articles are becoming more favorably disposed toward the Chinese. Or at least less critical. Is this censorship? Perhaps. Self-censorship? Definitely.

The other major English-language daily, with a considerably smaller circulation (55,000), is the *Hong Kong Standard*, published by the Sing Tao Press Group. When it was founded in 1949, it was close to Taiwan's Kuomintang, but it has grown notably closer to Beijing's authorities in the past few years.

In the local Chinese-language press, the most important dailies in terms of circulation are two popular publications. The *Oriental Daily News* (circulation, 400,000), founded in 1969 and directed by Lam Sun-choi, does not take any clear editorial stand. The *Apple Daily* (circulation, 300,000), owned by Jimmy Lai, is unashamedly sensationalist and anti-Communist.

A few others worth mention are *Sing Pao* (circulation, 190,000), whose autonomy has tended to crumble under Beijing's influence; *Ming Pao* (circulation, 110,000), probably the most respected for its independence; and *Wen Wei Po*, owned by the Chinese Communist Party (official circulation, 100,000).

On television, aside from American channels broadcast in China, there are two Hertzian channels. TVB, the most-watched station in Hong Kong, broadcasts in both languages: "Jade" in Chinese and

"Pearl" in English. ATV also broadcasts in both languages ("Home" and "World"). There is also a bilingual cable station, Wharf Cable.

Three satellite stations are also available: Star TV of the Murdoch Group, the China Entertainment Television Broadcast Limited (CETV), and Chinese Television Network, in which the Ming Pao Group holds the majority of shares and which was the first to announce Deng Xiaoping's death.

There are fifteen radio stations, including seven public stations under the auspices of Radio Television Hong Kong (RTHK), founded in 1929. These seven stations offer the full gamut of programs. Channel 2 broadcasts in Cantonese for young people, Channel 3 offers local news in English, Channel 4 is for classical music, 5 is geared toward minorities, 6 broadcasts the BBC World Service, and 7 is a music station.

POLITICAL FREEDOM

The End of the Democratic Movement of 1989
1989. After the massacre in Beijing's Tiananmen Square, the people of Hong Kong protested the repression in mainland China by the tens of thousands. There were unprecedented demonstrations.

Under the banner of the Hong Kong Alliance in Support of the Patriotic Democratic Movement in China, processions and rallies were organized, a statue of Miss Democracy was erected, and the Chinese Communist Party was booed and vilified.

Ieoh Ming Pei, architect of the Pyramid of the Louvre and creator of the famous seventy-two-story steel-and-glass Bank of China building which dominates the island, asked publicly: Should collaborations with the Beijing regime continue?

On the port, facing the Star Ferry on Statue Square, the granite memorial to the World War II dead was transformed into a flower-strewn monument of silent prayer and solidarity with the students of Beijing.

Suddenly the island came out of its torpor. The image of the Chinese army's brutality, broadcast live on television screens, aroused a dormant sense of magnanimity among the inhabitants of Hong Kong, who until then had been preoccupied by more mercenary concerns. This mercantile port became humanized by its solidarity with a struggling youth crushed by rows of tanks. The people cried out their indignation!

And then—nothing, or nearly nothing. The clamor died down. The demonstrators folded up their banners. Over the years that followed, protest movements against the excesses of the Chinese dictatorship have been few and far between. A few gatherings here and there in Victoria Park, with the traditional white memorial candles, occasional demonstrations in front of the New China Agency over the arrest of a dissident in mainland China.

On the eve of reunification, only a few dozen still rallied around the shrunken flag of democracy. There was a longer line in front of the United States consulate, people hoping for an American visa, than there was in front of the New China Agency.

Martin Lee and Emily Lau

"It's because the people are afraid," explained Martin Lee in February 1997, as if to reassure himself. Lee is president of the Democratic Party, the most important political organization in Hong Kong, and the winner by a landslide of the 1995 legislature elections, with 85% of the vote.

Martin Lee, along with Emily Lau, is one of Hong Kong's last political figures to struggle for the preservation of democracy in Hong Kong. He is one of the rare ones who ultimately did not collaborate with the Chinese officials.

Born in Hong Kong in 1938 and a graduate of the universities of Hong Kong and London, Martin Lee has the look of a martyr, but he talks like a man of law. He has an emaciated face, with the eyes of an abused puppy behind large glasses. He is always dressed soberly in a dark suit.

Elected a deputy in 1991 and 1995, he warned relentlessly —and in vain—of the dangers of communism. Little by little the crowds of his followers diminished. A few months before the handover, he was a preacher without a congregation.

His message lost its force rapidly abroad as well. In early 1997 he undertook a European tour to persuade heads of state to intervene so that People's China would respect its obligation to change nothing in the system for a period of fifty·years. He was given a polite reception, nothing more. In France Jacques Chirac, whom he had known since Chirac was mayor of Paris, did not receive him. He was met instead by Minister of Justice Jacques Toubon.

The comforting words he heard in Europe did not convince him. Mr. Lee is not naive. He knows that the countries of the West—all of them—have only one idea in their heads: to get a foothold in People's China and its market of more than a billion consumers. Human rights come in second to commerce.

Emily Lau is also well aware of this bitter fact. An attractive, distinguished woman, often dressed in Chanel suits, she was born in Hong Kong in 1952. Tenacious and ready to fight, she believes in Hong Kong as a nation with all her heart—and with a good deal of naiveté—and loathes the English as much as she does the Communist Chinese. Emily Lau repudiates both the Great Colonizer, so out of touch with its colonies, and the officials of Beijing, promoters of an unjust totalitarian system. Her dream is that Hong Kong will become an independent country.

A former journalist, Lau was a production assistant for BBC in London before successfully heading the prestigious *Far Eastern Review* in Hong Kong. On December 19, 1984, Margaret Thatcher signed the Joint Declaration with the Chinese, and some time later gave a press conference. Emily Lau, still a reporter, leapt up and lashed out at the Prime Minister in the presence of her astounded colleagues: "How dare you present yourself before the people of Hong Kong, after sealing their fate without consulting them?"

Thatcher was taken aback. A major politician was born: Emily Lau, elected to Parliament in 1991 and 1995 in the East division of the New Territories, has not ceased struggling for the rights of her fellow citizens. Right to the end, she would gladly exchange her suit for jeans and a T-shirt to protest in front of the New China Agency and challenge the police to arrest her.

Like her friend Martin Lee, she believes fear of China's repressive politics has driven the inhabitants of the island into complacency since the dissolution of the Parliament elected in 1995 or after the abolition of laws guaranteeing the right of free assembly. Of course, fear has probably played a role. But it is not the only reason.

The other reason—a plausible one—is that the people of Hong Kong were not sufficiently attached to the British system, despite its recent overtures, to fight for it in the street and provoke a violent reaction from their future governors. Lau reiterates, and with good reason, that the English, after all, waited 139 years to begrudgingly accord the first partial elections of the legislature.

It was too little, too late. The direct vote was for only one-third of the seats on the Legislative Council. After much wavering, the English in 1995 adopted a complex system to designate the thirty members of the Legislative Council: twenty members elected by popular vote across the territory; thirty from constituent bodies representing the various economic, social, and professional sectors, and ten elected by an Election Committee Constituency, which in turn is elected by the members of the district committees.

So, one might well ask how things might have turned out if the English had not stalled for so long in giving Hong Kong universal suffrage. Thanks to England's tardiness, the Chinese have a perfect excuse to replace the elected Parliament with an appointed chamber. "We agreed in 1984 not to change anything in the system in force," they remind the world. "Since the vote dates from 1990, six years later, we therefore are not bound to respect it."

During the weeks preceding the arrival of the Chinese, at any rate, she was not idle. She was seen before all the TV cameras of the world, heard on all the radio stations, repeating the same speech of solidarity in the face of the Chinese—and the English—with exemplary courage and determination.

What Happened to the Dissidents of Tienanmen?

Between five hundred to one thousand dissidents found refuge in Hong Kong, some of them after having spent several years in Chinese jails. Grace (a pseudonym), born in 1964, was among them. At fifteen she led a group of teenagers who distributed information on the Democracy movement in her small home town in the southern part of China.

Found guilty of espionage and "counterrevolutionary" acts, she was condemned to six years of imprisonment. During this period she was shuttled from farms in far-flung corners of the country to miserable prison cells in cities.

"I can remember being so hungry sometimes," she recalled, "that I mistook my pillow for a piece of bread."

Today Grace, a gaunt-faced wisp of a woman not quite five feet tall, has turned her life around in Hong Kong. She is married and works as editor-in-chief of a magazine, but repudiates none of her recent past. She writes regularly for magazines hostile to Beijing and participates in all the protests.

"I do not believe." she says, "that the Communists will respect the slogan 'One country, two systems.' I think that they will continue to repress freedom of expression. It's so much a part of their nature that they will want to crush anyone who opposes the regime!"

Grace wants to leave. She requested a visa for the United States, but months before the handover, had yet to receive a reply. "I hope that I won't be here by July first," she said.

But not everyone is in the same situation. The majority of dissidents of Tienanmen who took refuge in Hong Kong have abandoned politics altogether—some are disillusioned, others need to work. These are the well-behaved ones, cast in the same mold. Many of them now regularly cross the Chinese border on business trips with valid Hong Kong passports. Tienanmen is a thing of the past for them.

The best-known of the dissidents who wish to stay in Hong Kong, Han Dongfang, attempted to create a workers' union based on Poland's Solidarity. After the Movement of 1989 he spent twenty-two months in prison in China before being freed for medical reasons and sent to the United States. "I don't want to leave my country any more," he says proudly.

Only about forty refugees are seeking a safe conduct to leave again. Ten or so countries have offered to receive them, but on one condition: that they come discreetly, avoiding all publicity. The West is certainly generous, but it does not want to jeopardize its business interests in the People's Republic of China.

What Role Will the Communist Party Play?

This is a well-kept secret: What role does the Chinese Communist Party intend to play in the future?

During the last forty years of the British administration it maintained the lowest possible profile, limiting its activities to throwing oil on the fire, in the worst of cases, to prevent the English from colonizing in peace. This was especially true of the 1967 uprisings. Although the Party could have taken part in the legislature elections belatedly held by the British, it "forgot" to list itself among the territory's political parties. It remains hidden.

Officially, then, the Chinese Communist Party as such has never really existed in Hong Kong. But today, under the Communist regime, how will it evolve? Will it finally come out in broad daylight? Probably not. In order not to frighten investors, it will remain in the shadows, pulling the strings without ever appearing. This is a setup that it especially prefers.

This quite controversial question of the Party's role in Chinese Hong Kong prompted Tung's first political *faux pas*. A few days before his nomination, on November 20, 1996, he announced before the World Economic Forum that the Communist Party's status would be legalized.

"The Communist Party will have a legal existence in Hong Kong after June 30, 1997," he stated before an audience of concerned business executives.

Since then, Tung has changed his mind; or rather, it was changed for him. Because for the moment the Chinese officials intend to leave things as they are. The Communist Party prefers secrecy over public honors.

In the past few years, various members of Parliament have attempted to open up a debate on the issue. But it was always cut short. The members never manage to find a quorum to place it on the agenda, and it is always tabled indefinitely.

Deputy Christine Loh regularly posed the following question to the tribune of the Assembly. On March 6, 1997 she asked: "When the colonial era is over, how will we be able to pretend that the Communist Party doesn't exist and that it isn't interested in Hong Kong?"

How could anyone not be aware that the party will be the de facto master of the island? Beijing always hides behind the all-purpose slogan "One country, two systems." The Chinese Communists swear that the intervention of the government and of the party will be limited to the two spheres "reserved" to them by the Basic Law: foreign affairs and national defense.

Besides, Beijing points out, the Communist Party enjoys no particular power in this law, a mini-Constitution of sorts. This is true. But Hong Kong's recent history indicates that the Communists have always been present, even if they remain in the shadows.

The Communist Party's Role During the 1967 Uprisings

The Communists' role in the uprisings that broke out in 1967 is, in this sense, typical. In 1945, after World War II, Hong Kong's economic situation was hardly bright after three years and eight months of Japanese occupation. Business had practically disappeared; the currency was losing much of its value; and food was growing short. The population had increased from 460,000 in 1946 to nearly 2 million a year later, as refugees poured in from mainland China.

Starting in 1948, with the civil war in China, the population grew even more. Hong Kong was inundated with immigrants. The 1950s became the Nightmare Years.

Only the arrival of people from Shanghai allowed Hong Kong to take the upper hand again, a fact that Tung Chee-hwa, himself a Shanghai native, will point out privately.

Many of these new arrivals were textile workers, who virtually brought the industry with them in their suitcases. The industrial revolution was born. By early 1960 the territory had put its problems behind it and was beginning to make money.

This was too much for the followers of the Cultural Revolution and the partisans of the cult of Mao. From January to April 1967 riots broke out, directed from afar by various local Communist organizations, trade unions and teachers' groups. Bombs exploded at the Chinese border, leaving 51 dead and 832 wounded.

Officially, the party had no legal presence, but it showed how deeply it was enmeshed in Hong Kong's population.

While China's own prime minister, Zhou Enlai, consistently

affirmed in Beijing that the Cultural Revolution could not be exported, and many mainland businessmen, concerned for their businesses, did everything to avoid the crisis, the Communist Chinese of Hong Kong, playing on the nationalism of the island's inhabitants, showed their resolve and ability to cause unrest in the territory.

Things have calmed down since then, and party sympathizers have noticeably muted their demonstrations. Most of them have joined the pro-Chinese Democratic Alliance for the Betterment of Hong Kong, a political party headed by members of the Chinese Communist party. Its leader from the time of the 1967 uprisings, Tsang Yok Sing, took refuge in Canada after condemning the repression of the Democratic movement on Tienanmen Square.

In the early 1980s the Communist party in Hong Kong had six thousand members, according to the New China Agency. According to Emily Lau, they number ten thousand or more.

Soon the Chinese Communist party will naturally expand its influence in this recovered territory. There is just one unknown: How will the Party spread its net? If it affirms its usual bureaucratic and authoritarian practices, it will have a run-in with the people of the territory, accustomed as they are to freedom. Who knows? History might take its revenge, and the rebels of yesteryear might turn against the Communist party.

FREEDOMS FOR EXPATRIATES

Hong Kong is a dream. For foreigners it is even better—it is the embodiment of a dream. It is a vibrant territory, throbbing with life, where anything is possible, where life flows by simply and gaily, thanks to the stock market. It hardly seems real.

First of all, the geography is convenient. Everything is close at hand. The business center is located downtown, in the Central district, where merchants are clustered together—jewelers in one neighborhood, antique dealers in another—like a small provincial town.

Transportation is modern, fast, and efficient. The subway is a masterpiece, stretching forty-three kilometers and serving the island itself and, through a tunnel under the sea, the New Territories, right up to the Chinese border. The subway, or MTR (Mass Transit Railway), carries 2.5 million passengers each day in air-conditioned comfort. It is one of the busiest subways in the world.

Taxis are easy to find and inexpensive. And one should not fail to mention the quaint old painted trams or the ferries, old green-and-white tubs that constantly shuttle between Hong Kong and the mainland before the panorama of ultramodern skyscrapers towering on the hillside. It is like Manhattan transported to the tropical heat of Asia.

The old junks, unfortunately, are slowly disappearing. The few still in operation are renovated and belong to multinational corporations such as Paribas or Nestlé. In order to strike deals, these companies think it is essential to take their clients on a cruise around the great islands of the South China Sea.

Those fond of traditional China can wander through the neighborhoods of Wanchai or Mongkok. You can spend a few hours slumming in the harsh reality of the ghettos and then take refuge in the sumptuous villas of the Peak or the gorgeous apartment buildings of Mid Levels.

Those who appreciate American-style consumer society can window-shop in some of the most modern shopping centers in the world: Pacific Place or Times Square. They have everything in luxurious profusion, from French hairdressers to Japanese supermarkets. There are the tearooms of five-star hotels, as well as three-fork and six-baguette restaurants. A surfeit of choices!

Hong Kong is a corner of the globe where life is easy for rich expatriates. The world of commerce is always present, but not intrusive.

At nightfall, after the last cocktail party, after the final dinner party, wealthy whites go off in one direction, rich Asians in another.

The south of the island has superb broad and peaceful beaches. You can walk along the sea for miles on a pedestrian path. Except for two details—sharks from May to October; and the abominable Chinese custom of dumping everything into the sea. The water is often filthy in summer. Few Westerners dare go in deeper than their toes.

Golf, High Society, and Private Clubs

Imagine yourself on Repulse Bay Road, the thoroughfare crowning the southern residential district of Hong Kong. You are in a fabulous apartment building for rich expats and tycoons. From atop the twelfth floor John G. is nursing a glass of beer as he contemplates the bay. The calm sea glimmers with the silvery reflection of the moon. Below you can see the swimming pool and tennis courts. Farther off is a superb golf course. Still farther away, atop a hill, you can see Ocean Park, a marine theme park accessible by cablecar.

The forty-five-year-old John G. lives like a nabob. He prefers to remain anonymous. But his name is not important. Identities change, but the lifestyle remains the same.

His apartment is spacious, about two hundred square meters. It has four beautiful bedrooms overlooking the South China Sea and an American-style kitchen. He has access to a minibus service which takes him downtown.

What is the rent? $100,000 HK per month. That is a typical rent for luxury neighborhoods. Many people were expecting real-estate prices to drop after the departure of the British. Alas, they rose even higher. Speculation has continued to grow. Just before the 1997 handover, the wealthiest mainland Chinese rushed to buy up the last available apartments, either as living spaces or investments, fueling the fire.

It is the same story for rentals. There is a huge demand, backed by enormous capital, for a limited supply of space. Skyscrapers have proliferated like mushrooms, but soon there will not be enough land left to put in another building among the ones that are already built. Every six months a new building springs up on the Peak. The skyscrapers look like spikes poking through the mountain's skirt.

In 1997, only a few square inches of undeveloped land was left. The natives of Hong Kong have seen their city devoured by concrete as their eardrums have been burst by jackhammers. The few pedestrians must have a death wish. Sidewalks, where they exist at all, are hardly more than a few centimeters wide, just enough to allow people to avoid being mowed down by traffic. In this country, where the size and make of a car correspond to its owner's social class, the roads leading up the Peak are terribly narrow. Buses graze each other, and the limousines are barely able to pass each other. But apartment buildings are still springing up.

John is happy. Who wouldn't be? He earns a fabulous salary. As is the case with all expatriates in the upper echelons of business, his company graciously pays for his apartment, a car, and an annual trip to Europe for him and his family. The company also gives him free membership to one of the several private clubs—very exclusive, in the British style. In his case, the Hong Kong Club.

These clubs are part of Hong Kong's culture. Top decision-makers take their meals, play squash, and have a massage after going to the sauna. It is a custom inherited from the British. How many contracts have been signed in these luxurious jewel boxes, protected from the outside world, where one speaks in hushed tones? Good food, sports, and luxury keep the wheels of commerce turning.

These clubs demand exorbitant membership fees. Oddly, this is one of the reasons for their success. The clubs with the highest prices are the ones where the membership is most highly coveted—typical of the snobbery of Hong Kong's haute bourgeoisie.

For example, the China Club occupies the top three floors of the

Old Bank of China Building. It has a magnificent setting and a library filled with old Chinese books, many of them antique, on all aspects of cultural and artistic life.

On the fifteenth floor five private suites are open twenty-four hours a day for playing cards and *mahjong*. Membership fees are as high as $150,000 HK and monthly dues are $880 HK. At the Chinese restaurant the French consul rubs elbows with the local financial executives. Heirs of old British families clink glasses with powerful bankers.

As for foreign journalists, you can find them at the Foreign Correspondents' Club (FCC) on Lower Albert Road. It has two restaurants, a gym, and a workroom equipped with several computers, and, of course, a great bar on the ground floor. On Friday night underneath the fans, the FCC is the official meeting place for reporters passing through the area. The membership fees are not as steep as in other clubs: $750 HK per month for journalists and considerably more for others—for example, businessmen who wish to mix with newsmen; or foreigners who cannot afford to join the Hong Kong Club.

And there are the countless golf clubs. These magnificent green spaces escape being devoured by concrete for a reason—many of their richest members are real-estate dealers. The clubs offer superb greens and mind-boggling membership fees.

Finally, there are establishments reserved for women. The men working in Hong Kong often need to travel. They scour the region and spend hardly more than a few days each month on the island. They need to keep their wives amused. At the Ladies Recreation Center, for example, on Old Peak Road, they can swim in the pool, take a sauna, play bridge or tennis, and take tea. The membership rates are extremely high, and the waiting list incredibly long. But the companies pay, and the expenses are tax-deductible.

John, for one, does not care for high society. You never see his picture in the chic society pages. The typical subjects you see, usually holding glasses of champagne in their hands, are more often merchants or diplomats from the Western consulates.

After work, John spends time with his family when he can, and thinks about his vacation. Winter in Sapporo, Japan, autumn on a beach in the Philippines or Thailand, summer in Europe. . . . All these expatriate businessmen live more or less the same—in luxury.

John represents one of the most prestigious insurance agencies in the world. Insurance is a highly developed field in Hong Kong, with no fewer than 221 companies, of which 121 are registered outside the territory. According to official statistics, premiums total about $40 billion HK. This success can be explained by the use of long-term policies, Hong Kong's meager social security coverage, the high price of medical care, and the fact that state pensions are administered through private companies.

John is one of the fifty thousand British who still live in Hong Kong. Many have already left. In the census taken in late 1995, continental Europeans and Americans numbered 307,900, or 28% of the population.

The Luxury Sector: The Garment Industry and High Fashion

The luxury sector is in fine form, oozing more money than any other field. The big fashion houses have hardly been affected by the counterfeit brands sold in abundance in the crowded alleys of the Mongkok district or Tsim Sha Tsui. The bootleg brands are manufactured in China and South Korea. Each market caters to its own clientele: imi-tations for tourists, originals for rich natives and foreigners. Not far from Hermès, in front of Versace on Des Voeux Road, you can watch an amusing ballet of Mercedes, Rolls, and BMW limousines turning slowly around the neighborhood while their mistresses finish their shopping.

Hong Kong is the Asia's window on fashion. The Japanese and South Koreans charter entire Boeings to seek out the newest creations of the great couturiers. They strip bare the racks of Galeria, Prince's Building, and other luxury shopping centers located in the magnificent apartment buildings of Central.

Clothing is on the top of tourists' shopping lists and has represented a major part of Hong Kong's economy since its beginnings. According to a March 1996 study by the Poste d'Expansion Economique Français, 3,500 establishments employed a total of 70,000 people in this field, in spite of the relocation phenomenon of the 1980s.

Because of its status as a free port, all fashion merchandise that enters the territory is exempt from customs duties. China, Hong Kong's number one business partner, accounts for ninety percent of the island's imports.

Traders and Promotional Gifts

The appointments are usually made in the lobbies of big hotels, for example, today in the Mandarin Oriental: "I'm blond, with curly hair. I'll be wearing a leather jacket."

At the appointed hour, Fred Garnett enters the lobby of the palace as promised.

Not quite thirty years old, with a strong British accent, Fred Garnett is one of the countless traders who comb Hong Kong's market. There is nothing mysterious about his work, and certainly nothing illegal. Many of his colleagues, like him, are young people concerned by the unemployment rate in Europe. They boldly come to Hong Kong to launch careers as intermediaries between the Asian market and the West.

For example, say you sell camping equipment or artificial flowers in France and you want to import these products from China at the lowest prices available. People like Fred Garnett will search out the articles you want and deliver them to you directly.

One of the biggest French department stores, for instance, created its own children's backpack label, which is manufactured in mainland China, through a young trader. This thirtyish woman has been established here for seven years. She does brisk business and does not hide the fact that she has a fat bank account.

Here is another example: You are looking for promotional gifts for your company: cigarette lighters, T-shirts, watches, radios. All the junk, all the gadgets generously distributed throughout the world by companies for promotional reasons, often pass through Hong Kong. No problem. Fred Garnett will help you avoid all the hassles of shipping and customs. He knows where to find the comb or the sandals which will bear your logo.

For the most part these promotional items are no longer manufactured in Hong Kong; they only pass through in transit. In 98% of cases they are assembled in mainland China, especially in the southern regions of Canton and Shenzhen. More than ten years ago, Hong Kong relocated its factories, essentially becoming a center for services.

So how does Fred Garnett track down the products that will be sold later in Europe or elsewhere?

"I consult *Enterprise*, the businessman's bible in Hong Kong," he answers softly.

Enterprise is a thick and lavish magazine published by the Hong Kong Trade Development Council, an official organization. It features eight hundred pages of drawings and photographs of all the items on sale for export.

This is where Fred Garnett and his colleagues get their ideas. The foreign buyers who use their services could very well read *Enterprise* and directly contact the manufacturers or exporters themselves. They are aware of this. For the sake of convenience and speed, however, they rely on traders instead.

Fred Garnett's work is not always a stroll on the beach. Once the contract is signed, he has to guarantee the product after the sale. Imagine a contract for three thousand watches. He has to oversee production, visit the factory several times, and make sure the watches are flawless. And in mainland China, manufacturing often leaves quite a bit to be desired.

"I've already had to ask several times that a product be remade," he said. "For example, once I had ordered hair brushes, and they made combs." The Chinese will usually agree to redo a defective order, willingly if not graciously.

Once the merchandise is received in China the trader has to go through the mystifying maze of administration and customs that precedes shipping. This is the prelude to the final act—the delivery of the product to the West.

These traders, in the final analysis, are well paid. For example, our guide Fred earns a respectable $40,000-plus HK per month.

"What I miss the most," he said, "are friends and meeting places. The beaches are polluted, and the city is small."

Lan Kwai Fong: Contrescarpe, Hong Kong Style

Young expatriates inevitably start out in the Lan Kwai Fong district, next to D'Aguilar Street. It is a neighborhood of four or five small pedestrian streets similar to the Contrescarpe area in Paris. Before it became the meeting place of night owls it had been Hong Kong's central trash-collection point. Now it is a center of pleasure, like Les Halles in Paris.

On Saturday night the pavement is crowded with red-faced Golden Boys, mainly English and Australian, their shirts unbuttoned after work, beers in their hands. Bars such as San Francisco are too small, so they drink in crowds on the sidewalk in the heat of the night. Later they will finish their evening in a club, such as the Jazz Club or 1997. This cramped space is frequented by the whitest and the richest. Dior bags compete with Chanel suits. The expats scope one another.

The neighborhood, with its dozens of bars and fashionable restaurants, is almost exclusively frequented by Westerners. Asians hardly ever show their faces. It is the quarter for expats on the binge. Realtors mingle with fashion executives. They spend their fat commissions on products which are sometimes manufactured by the young heirs of corrupt Communism and bought on the mainland for a pittance, then sold at twice the price in the West.

In Lan Kwai Fong, China seems a million miles away. A McDonalds looks down its nose at a pizzeria and a Lebanese restaurant. It is a tiny oasis of eating places and clubs for expatriates, a paradise owned by a clever man, Allan Zeman.

His resume lists him as the president of more than half a dozen companies. He is a Canadian, a millionaire several times over, who drives around town in a Bentley. An elegant balding man of about fifty, he is always dressed in a silk shirt with a Mao collar. He made his fortune in the garment industry before becoming the Régine of Hong Kong. He is on the A-list for all high-society events in the city.

Allan Zeman will tell anyone who cares to listen that he is sanguine about Hong Kong's future. In "his" zone he fills the little remaining space with new apartment buildings or new restaurants. Even better, he has decided to build an exact copy of "his" Lan Kwai Fong in Canton. But, like a good businessman, he does not keep all his eggs in one basket. He has huge investments in both Canada and Australia.

Tourism: The Hotel Peninsula and Its Stars

It would be impossible to write about the Hong Kong of the rich without devoting a few words to the famous Hotel Peninsula—a symbol of wealth and decadent colonialism.

The "Pen," as its habitués call it, faces the island of Hong Kong from Kowloon. It opened on December 11, 1928, with three thousand guests in attendance, and quickly became the meeting place for high society and a temple of gossip. The rooms of the Peninsula are rarely taken by unknowns; past guests include Julie Andrews, William Holden, Candice Bergen, Cary Grant, Elton John, Roman Polanski, Elizabeth Taylor, Ronald Reagan, and Gilbert Bécaud.

Kowloon's Mega-Nightclubs

The richest people of Hong Kong gather late at night in Kowloon's Las Vegas-style nightclubs: BBOSS, Lost in the City, and China City. Kowloon is a "must" stop for moneyed revelers. They are gigantic, vulgarly sumptuous clubs, as large as warehouses. The filtered light of the dance floor contrasts with the aggressive multicolor neon of the stage lights. You see fountains here, reconstructions of Roman palaces there—American-style luxury reinterpreted by Hong Kong designers. All these clubs put on an elaborate show with sequins galore and semi-nude Western girls. The volume is pushed up to the max, the dancers are gorgeous, and the drinks are expensive.

Lonely guests, if they so desire, may treat themselves to the company of a charming hostess. At Lost in the City the price is $400 HK per hour. At China City it is $56 HK for ten minutes. Two hundred professionals—English, Japanese, or Thai, each one sexier than the last—work almost the whole night through. If the consumer does not care for the girl he is assigned, he can have her exchanged in ten minutes. And if he wants to take her elsewhere? No problem. He has only to pay an "exit fee," which is usually several hundred dollars!

The cognac and champagne flow freely. The tourists and expatriates have a hard time keeping up with the local tycoons. A night out can easily cost between $1,000 and $2,500 US!

SEXUAL FREEDOM

You know the place by the green neon lights. It is called the Caprice Bar. It is one of the countless karaoke bars that have opened in the past few years in Shenzhen, in the province of Guangdong. Shenzhen is two hours by train from Hong Kong. It was the first of five "Special Economic Zones" in southern China, enclaves conceived in the late 1970s by Deng Xiaoping.

Shenzhen—Deng's Baby and China's Garbage Dump

Shenzhen, with a population that rose from 70,000 in 1978 to 3.5 million today, is the life-size laboratory of a Socialist China breathlessly open to the capitalist market.

In February 1992, on a tour of the south intended to boost production and conscious of the disastrous state of the existing system, Deng praised the market economy and advocated certain elements of capitalism. Upon his death in February 1997, thousands of grateful Chinese, breaking with official orders, spontaneously placed wreaths before a giant photograph of Deng in the center of town—a poster depicting him emerging from a sky-blue background before ultramodern factories and skyscrapers. The father of the Chinese economy surging to the zenith of his creation!

Since the handover of Hong Kong to China, the officials of Shenzhen plan to erect a life-size bronze bust of their illustrious benefactor. It is the least they can do!

Now, Shenzhen is a stinking hole with horrendous architecture, dotted with housing projects. It owes everything to Deng Xiaoping.

In fifteen years, thanks to its bold economic feats, Shenzhen enjoyed a dizzying boom. In less than five years it jumped merrily from the Third World to become an ultramodern society. The growth of its gross domestic product (GDP) is calculated at 36%; between 1992 and 1994, the GDP doubled.

Shenzhen is a bridge between the twenty-first century and a China that is still backward in many respects. It is a megalopolis with a dual role: an industrial center for the rest of China and a fabulous showcase intended to attract billions of dollars in foreign investments. Hong Kong owes much to Shenzhen—it relocated most of its factories there in the late 1980s.

The region's rapid development can be explained by its tax benefits (a rate of fifteen percent on revenues, as opposed to thirty-three percent for the rest of the country), tax exemption for profits reinvested, and also from import taxes for production equipment and raw materials. Finally, companies are not required to pay taxes on their profits for their first two years, and they receive a fifty percent reduction for the next two years.

Over the years, the town has exploded. The Chinese have come from the most far-flung provinces to strike it rich in this El Dorado, as Deng encouraged them. Without much persuasion, they came in hordes. Money became their Number One priority, their only reason to live—to the point that the frenzied race for dollars has threatened the regime's stability.

On the other side of the coin, though, the flourishing economy has given birth to three major social vices: crime, corruption, and prostitution. This is a trio inherent in Deng's system which could well pollute Hong Kong in the years to come.

Nothing is ever built any more in Shenzhen without bribes. Under-the-table deals are what keep the economy moving.

Here dollars, rather than the yuan, China's national currency, are used. Shenzhen is a country within a country!

What a difference from Hong Kong! Shenzhen is China's "Far Southeast," the land of cowboys. Beijing seems so far away. The most basic laws do not exist here—of course, this is a phenomenon common throughout China, but it is multiplied many times over in Shenzhen. Delinquency is increasing to dangerous levels. Beggars crowd the sidewalks near the bus and train stations. Arriving from

Hong Kong, the culture shock is incredible. You pass directly from a city that is beautiful, clean, orderly and modern, to one that is ugly, dirty and menacing. As soon as you step off your train you are surrounded by street urchins in rags. Everywhere you see signs advertising massage parlors with dubious sanitary conditions. In the street, girls dressed as bellhops accost tourists to lead them to apartments crowded with prostitutes, usually young girls from the street. At prices to beat all the competition.

Like other Special Economic Zones, Shenzhen is one of mainland China's garbage dumps, a center of debauchery ready to invade Hong Kong. When the British controlled Hong Kong they scrupulously observed the quotas of Chinese allowed to cross the border (150 persons daily), as well as the status and authenticity of their working papers. In the future, the door to enter Hong Kong will be wide open. . . .

A Cognac in the Karaoke Bar: Return of the Concubines

On Saturday night the Caprice Bar is packed. Not a single stool is available. The VSOP cognac flows freely. As is often the case in Asia, people are mixing it with . . . Coca-Cola or tonic water!

The Chinese girls, in their black leather miniskirts and body stockings, are gorgeous. The small private rooms have all been booked for several days. It is the weekend, and in the cigarette smoke, Shenzhen is partying. The vast majority of the clients, their pockets stuffed with dollars, come from Hong Kong by train or bus.

Karaoke is Asia's pastime. The amateur sings in playback in front of a silent television screen on which he sees the words to the song. Microphone in hand, he takes himself for Michael Jackson. He is a star for the night. A girl is at his side, urging him to drink. This is the ugly face of capitalism.

Sin has been working at the Caprice for two years. Officially her job is limited to singing with the customers and making them feel comfortable so they will order more drinks. After closing time, if the client is nice, she will spend the rest of the night with him for a few hundred dollars.

But Sin wants something more from life. Like most of her girlfriends in the south, a region flush with easy money, what she would like to find is a man who would choose her as his mistress.

Concubinage, a custom nearly as old as China itself, is making a comeback in a big way.

As for Tina, she is overjoyed. She has finally found a soulmate to pay her bills. A certain Chan, a bus driver, pays her rent. Even better, he gives her $4,000 a month on one condition—that she give up her work in the karaoke bar. "My life has become more stable," she whispers. "I've stopped being nervous every night at the thought of not getting clients or getting beat up by a drunken stranger."

There are other examples. Jessie, who I met at a fast-food restaurant in Shenzhen, is quite proud of her situation:

"My boyfriend is married with two children in Hong Kong. What harm is there in that? As long as he's nice to me and he helps me make ends meet and pays the rent, that's enough!"

One Country, Two Families

Their apartment is in the center of town. On the chest in the living room, he has placed a photo of his legal wife. He gives his family in Hong Kong half of his salary, about $20,000 HK a month.

This man and his mistress have everything a young couple could dream of: a color television, a VCR, records, a dishwasher. All the modern conveniences.

Jessie, however, is not faithful. Yes, she has left the karaoke bar as her boyfriend asked, but secretly she continues to do what she calls "part-time" work: $300 HK for a visit, $600 HK for the night.

Eliza is twenty-three. She left Jiangsu, her native province in eastern China, two years ago. She asks for between $800 and $1,000 for a visit and $15,000 for the night.

She is gorgeous, and very popular in the bar. The conversation quickly takes a conventional turn. The journalist/client, passing himself off as a textile executive, asks how much it would cost to "keep" her—the time-honored formula for finding a concubine—and how much to find another girl for his boss. Eliza's interest perks up remarkably.

She lives in an apartment in the Jak Hing Building, close to the station. The rent for her three-room apartment is $7,200. For $15,000 a month, she would do anything.

"For that amount of money, I guarantee you I won't sleep with other men, and I won't do any more part-time. I will wait for you every day. You can come when you want. I will be your servant!"

She makes you pity her. "You know, us girls from Jiangsu, we're honest and straight people. If you treat me good, I'll treat you even better. The main thing is, don't sleep with girls from the south. They'll rob you and bleed you dry!"

Eliza, her body poured into a satin dress, gets carried away. She offers the services of a friend who, like her, is looking for a "protector." "Sin Ming is about twenty and she's prettier than me, with big breasts. She works in the post office in my village. She has a great personality. I'll introduce you to her, and on your end, you'll introduce me to your boss. If it works out, she'll quit her job right away and she can be in Shenzhen in two or three weeks. She's very nice, very honest. She might even be a virgin. . . ."

Not far from Shenzhen there is a village called Wong Pui Ling, nicknamed "The Mistresses' Corner." During the week, oddly, you see only women. On Saturday night they walk with their boyfriends, who have left their families in Hong Kong.

Only one humanitarian agency, Caritas, tries to aid the *ta pan*, women with philandering husbands. The group of about twenty women meets once a week. Most of them are from the middle class. Their husbands are truck drivers, civil servants, or heads of small factories—men in their fifties earning about $10,000 a month.

The wives feel despair and anguish at the idea of being alone. Before turning to Caritas, they had hired private detectives to find out more about their husbands. This is often how a wife discovers her husband's double life.

"Nothing matters any more," says Molly. "Since he met that twenty-year-old girl in a karaoke bar our life is upside down. He goes to Shenzhen at least twice a week. He'll use any excuse—a childhood friend passing through, work, anything!"

Several of them have even discovered that their husbands have children across the border. For years they had been supporting two families. The wives never suspected a thing. They all tell the same story: They were happy and in love, until the other woman entered the scene. Many resign themselves to it. What else can they do? Most of them have no profession, no savings, and children to feed.

A Happy Concubine at Eighty-nine

Concubinage goes back to the time of the emperors. It has practically always existed in China. Until the 1940s, it was quite common for a man to have a concubine.

Pui-kwan, eighty-nine years of age, was born in Shun Tak, in Guangdong Province. This old woman, today nearly blind, laughs when you talk to her about women's liberation. She lived as a concubine for thirty-five years.

"I was perfectly happy," she recounts in her trembling voice. "For me it was a way to stay free and independent. I loved Kwok (the man who kept her) very much, but not enough to live by his side day and night. When he was with his wife I had the chance to take care of me!"

Her relationship with the legal wife was admirable. "She told me at the very beginning that we should understand each other like two sisters. And that's what happened! There was never any jealousy between us. We used to enjoy making fun of him, since we both knew him so well." Kwok's family, "treated me perfectly," she insists. "His mother told me never to let anyone look down on me. She was a great mother. . . ."

The three "legitimate" sons have always respected her as if she were their mother. "In 1957 I needed an operation and our eldest son donated his blood!" She says "our" son, even though she has never had a child.

Two Keys For
An Uncertain Future

AT THE END OF THE ROAD . . . TAIWAN

From the Communist party's point of view, the fates of Hong Kong and Taiwan are inextricable. It is impossible to determine the future of one and not the other. A serious error committed in the British colony after the handover could compromise reunification with Taiwan, which is considered by far Beijing's most important issue. The return to the fold of the little rich rebel, in secession since 1949, is the ultimate goal of the Communist heads of state. It consumes them considerably more than the future of the troublesome rock that is Hong Kong.

The Next Guinea Pigs

Consequently, the Taiwanese more than anyone else have their eyes riveted on the transition of Hong Kong. If everyone agrees that the attitude of the Chinese Communists in the former British colony is like a laboratory experiment, the next guinea pigs will be the Taiwanese.

Once Hong Kong has returned to the bosom of China, there will no longer be a barrier between Taiwan and People's China. It will be the last, elusive duckling which must sooner or later rejoin the flock.

When Deng Xiaoping created the slogan "One country, two systems" in 1981, it was Taiwan that he had in mind first before applying the ingenious slogan to Hong Kong.

For the moment there is no problem. Taiwan's economy, strongly linked with China's, inevitably passes through Hong Kong and by necessity will continue to do so in the absence of direct ties between the "two Chinas." In spite of the sounds of warships in the Strait of Formosa, in spite of the regular saber-rattling between Beijing and Taipei, commercial relations between the two countries are wonderfully stable. Taiwan's investments in China, estimated at more than $30 billion, pass through Hong Kong. Many Taiwanese manufacturers have their products assembled in China via the former English colony, which then re-exports them.

Taipei is represented in Hong Kong by hundreds of unofficial offices, the best known being the Chung Hwa Travel Service, which serves as a cover for the unofficial Taiwan Embassy. Its director is traditionally an employee of Taiwan's Ministry of Foreign Affairs.

Money Is Money: A Love-Hate Relationship

For the time being, Hong Kong's role of "bridge" between the two countries should not change. On the contrary. If Taiwan has a profound need for Hong Kong, similarly People's China has a vested interest in keeping the Taiwanese in Hong Kong. The commercial comings and goings are played out in both directions. Chinese airlines and freight carriers use Hong Kong as a stopover en route to Taiwan and vice versa. This will surely continue.

The situation is a kind of love-hate relationship. Just before the last threat of war, in early 1996, business and financial relations had never been better between the two enemy sisters: There are an estimated 2,000 Taiwanese companies in Hong Kong that work directly with the mainland. The majority of the 2 million Taiwanese who enter and leave Hong Kong each year are in transit to visit members of their families on the mainland. In June 1996, China's minister of foreign affairs, Qian Qichen, spelled out the upcoming relations between China and Taiwan. Unofficial contacts will continue, Taiwanese investments will be welcome and protected, and "special regional routes" by air and sea will be opened. If Taiwan does not commit what in Beijing's eyes would be the irreparable mistake of declaring its independence—which it will never do!—relations should remain as they are. In the press the Chinese and Taiwanese will open old wounds, but cloaked economic relations will continue to prosper. Money is money. This saying no doubt has deep roots in China.

But all is not rosy. Several Taiwanese businesses, nervous, have prudently made an escape plan. After the Chinese military exercises with real missiles and bullets in the Strait of Formosa in February 1996, they opened offices in the United States and Singapore—just in case the maneuvers should go past the intimidation stage.

The Retrenched Camp of Chiang Kai-Shek's Soldiers Abandoned to the Enemy

For the most part, however, Taiwan's businessmen are not too nervous about the future of Hong Kong. They predict it a prosperous fate as "the center for the future development of China," according to Chen Ding-kuo, a Taiwanese businessman quoted in the *Far Eastern Review*.

However, some of Hong Kong's thirty thousand Taiwanese residents are feeling uncomfortable: those who took refuge in the British colony after their defeat in 1949—Chiang Kai-shek's routed soldiers who did not manage to make their fortune and who are about to be condemned to live on enemy soil.

It is not so long ago that the red-and-blue nationalist flag floated proudly in front of their house. After the civil war they moved to Rennie Mills, a village in the eastern part of Kowloon, the "Little Taiwan" of Hong Kong. They lived there for close to fifty years, until the British colonizers decided in the summer of 1996 to close their village and to expel these "former" Taiwanese and relocate them in housing projects in different parts of the colony.

Officially, Rennie Mills was depopulated for real-estate reasons, to facilitate the construction of apartment buildings on the site. But many of the former soldiers doubt the truth of this explanation. They suspect the vengeful hand of Beijing. "The Communists wanted to separate us," says Li. "Together we were too dangerous! The English gave in to an order from Beijing." The English claim they acted in good faith.

Whatever the explanation, the facts are there. Despite their fierce resistance—one of them, Lau Ah Kouk, committed suicide by jumping out a window—the expelled Taiwanese have been diluted in the population. A dozen here, a dozen there. The colonial authorities apparently wanted to disperse them. They wouldn't have undertaken the plan otherwise.

In the whole territory, twenty thousand people have a Taiwan passport. For the most part, they have made up their minds to stay. Since 1949 these immigrants have started a new life. Their children have grown up in Hong Kong, and they have chosen Hong Kong as their new homeland. Despite their ever-strong loyalty to the Kuomintang—fifty years later—the Taiwanese have reluctantly chosen to mute their nationalism. They have nothing left except for a few moth-eaten flags, faded uniforms, and some out-of-date medals. For them, the war ended in 1949.

As for Taipei's authorities, they have adopted a prudent attitude in order to protect their sacrosanct bilateral commercial ties with

People's China. As of June 1996, they stopped paying the veterans residing in Hong Kong the modest pension of $360 HK a month. And they were hardly generous when they responded to the Rennie Mills evacuees' request for financial compensation. They gave a total of $6,500 HK for everyone.

TUNG CHEE-HWA, THE FIRST CHINESE GOVERNOR

Tung Chee-hwa, appointed by China as Hong Kong's first postcolonial chief executive, must have his own ideas about the sincerity of Beijing's leaders. Officially, he plays the "one country, two systems" card with a straight face, which is why he was chosen. He approaches his task with a zeal that astonishes even some officials close to Beijing.

He repeats the slogan at every opportunity. If we are to believe him, there is not the slightest cause for concern—the leaders of Beijing will respect Hong Kong's freedom as promised. In private, however, Tung Chee-hwa is naturally more circumspect, not offering any comments or raising any questions. He is obliged to remain reserved.

Tung Chee-hwa, or "C.H." as he is called by his friends, replaced Chris Patten at midnight on June 30, following in the footsteps of the man who conceived democratic reforms, albeit too late, when Hong Kong's fate was already sealed.

A powerfully built man with a boxer's physique, his white hair trimmed in a crew-cut, Tung rose to the highest public office at the age of sixty. He was born in Shanghai on May 29, 1937, the eve of the Japanese occupation of China—this is a point in his favor for the leaders of the regime, most of whom are also from Shanghai.

In Hong Kong, where business represents real power, he has an excellent pedigree as well. The son of a shipowner, he received an engineering degree in Liverpool, England. Later he worked for nearly ten years at General Electric in the United States.

Saved by Beijing Early in His Career
Upon his father's death in 1982, Tung took over the family's shipping business, Orient Overseas, Ltd., which was in desperate financial straits. It was the Communist Chinese who saved him from disaster—a fact he does not deny. The tycoon Henry Fok, who is well connected in Beijing, helped him avoid bankruptcy in 1985 by investing $120 million in his business, largely from mainland China.

Throughout his career, Tung Chee-hwa has been able to skillfully cultivate a variety of contacts. He has friendly ties with American Republicans, such as Henry Kissinger and George Bush, and has officially served as an advisor to British governor Chris Patten, all the while cultivating good relations with the Beijing regime.

Unlike the other tycoons, he is not fond of luxury. He has no interest in Rolls Royces, yachts or expensive properties. He is a solidly middle-class man with middle-class tastes. Before he was given the governor's three official cars, including a black Bentley, he drove a spacious but popular BMW (also black). Superstitious, like all Chinese, he chose not to live in the former home of the British governor because of its bad *feng shui*.

He has been faithfully married to his wife, Betty Chiu Hung-ping, since 1961 and together they have had three children. They continue to live in their own apartment. Measuring 180 square meters and decorated with paintings by Chinese masters from the nineteenth and twentieth centuries, it is located in the middle-class neighborhood of Mid Levels. He has a weekend home where he has built a karaoke room, a private movie theater, and a swimming pool for his family. He makes a point of devoting time especially for them.

As for his free time, he enjoys watching rugby—he is a fan of the Liverpool Football Club—and listening to the songs of Nat King Cole. These are two passions he acquired as a youth in Great Britain and later in the United States.

Can He Resist Beijing?

Several months before his nomination on December 11, 1996, by a four hundred-member "selection committee" handpicked by Beijing (he was its vice-president), there was no doubt that Tung would be named, because of a handshake that would become famous. In January of the same year, Chinese president Jiang Zemin reportedly approached him in the Palace of the People on Tienanmen Square to warmly shake his hand—the veritable emperor's blessing.

But how will this man, groomed by and beholden to Beijing, lead Hong Kong to the year 2000?

"The first year is the most important," Tung said in an interview published in the October 28, 1996 issue of the *South China Morning Post*. "It is necessary to act fast to win the confidence and support of the people of Hong Kong. And working together to win the confidence and respect of the central government [of Beijing] is absolutely crucial."

For the moment, Tung Chee-hwa has not caused any scenes. He has docilely upheld all the controversial dictates of Beijing.

In the "defense of Chinese values," the slogan he has adopted, he has approved the abolition of the elected Parliament (LEGCO) and its replacement by an appointed Provisional Legislature, as well as the amendment of certain laws dealing with human rights. Not a very auspicious start, from the democrats' point of view.

Will he be a reliable bastion of security in the face of Communist China's authoritarian rule? Or will he carry out Beijing's underhanded deals? Those who tend to believe the latter fear that Tung Chee-hwa is obliged to repay his debt to Beijing for saving his family's business from bankruptcy.

"What Hong Kong needs is not a spokesman for Beijing, but a leader who will defend its territory when the Chinese officials insist on interfering in its affairs," wrote Martin Lee, president of the Democratic Party, in an editorial published in the *Asian Wall Street Journal* on December 12, 1996.

Now that Tung Chee-hwa is governor, can he or will he play this role?

Conclusion

It's over—or, rather, it's just beginning. With three blasts of the trumpet, the Chinese national anthem erased a century and a half of British colonial rule. On June 30, 1997, Chris Patten, Prince Charles, and their guests in their Sunday best, embarked on the *Britannia*, accompanied by a handful of dethroned chieftains. One last admiring look at the bay, and the anchor was raised. The Chinese flag with its five yellow stars was hoised, forever sweeping away the Union Jack from official flagpoles.

Back on land, both of them clutching umbrellas in the tropical damp, Tung Chee-hwa gallantly saluted General Liu Zhenwu, commander of the First Regiment of the People's Liberation Army. The red flag—once and for all—flew over "the rock." London is dead, long live Beijing, capital of the Motherland! Long live Chinese Hong Kong!

Everyone had been waiting for that moment for thirteen years. There were no last-minute plot twists, everyone had plenty of time to prepare. The event was foreshadowed well in advance.

Yet, for all those years of preparation, when sovereignty was transferred we had little idea what the future of Hong Kong would hold.

Some imagined the mainland Chinese full of hatred and revenge, with knives between their teeth. Others thought that things were bound to remain unchanged for another fifty years. What suspense. All bets are on. Only one thing missing from this drama—the ending.

One year later, as these lines are written, we can see a little more clearly. But only a little.

So far, twelve months after the arrival of the Communists in Hong Kong, everything seems to suggest that those who predicted a gentle transfer of power were right.

Nothing in the streets suggests any drastic change. Everything is intact, preserved. The Chinese have proved more intelligent than their detractor chose to believe. Lurking in the shadows, they have not intervened—or hardly at all.

The people of Hong Kong have been vigilant. They have no intention of allowing their freedom to be lost in the corridors of Beijing. They have made this abundantly clear, on two occasions. On June 4, 1998, the ninth anniversary of the Tienanmen Square repression, and on May 20, 1998, during the first elections held since the transfer of power, the citizens of the "Special Administrative Region" clearly expressed their desire to maintain Deng Xiao Ping's well-known formula of "one country, two systems."

June 4, 1998. As if there had been no handover, as if there were no storm raging around them, tens of thousands of people crowded into Victoria Park, by candlelight. A year earlier, a few weeks before the transition, 55,000 people had gathered in the same park. Everyone was wondering whether the people of Hong Kong, once under Chinese rule, would still have the right to commemorate the deaths at Tienanmen. The answer was yes.

Almost as many people met on that historic fourth of June as had one year earlier. Better still, messages were read to the crowd from two dissidents loathed by Beijing, Wang Dan and Wei Jinsheng, who now live in the United States after their expulsion from the People's Republic. Thanks to the Internet, Wang Dan appeared on a giant television screen. A real event, unthinkable twelve months before. Throughout the demonstration, the police did not intervene. Beijing allowed it to take place.

Similarly, on May 20, 1998, the Chinese Communists did not prevent the people of Hong Kong from going to the polls as they had under British rule.

It is true that Beijing modified some aspects of the electoral law set up by the British. In particular, they introduced proportional representation, while the Crown had instituted the "first-past-the-post" system. This clever division, intended to facilitate the success of small political parties close to Beijing, did not have the intended result, however. The gerrymandering failed to prevent the democrats from winning 60% of the vote at this referendum, the first ever under the Chinese administration.

That Sunday, the vote took place under genuine scrutiny. Once again, however, there was no turmoil. Save the changes in the electoral system, the election took place as it had in previous years. The people of Hong Kong democratically elected one-third of the sixty deputies who sit in the Chamber, as was the case under British administration. The other two-thirds are appointed either by electoral colleges, now carefully chosen by those friendly to Beijing, or by representatives of various professions.

On election day, the weather was terrible. Rain, squalls, floods, landslides. But, like the Victoria Park demonstrators, the voters were not put off by the furies of Mother Nature. On the contrary—voter participation reached an unprecedented 53.3% of Hong Kong's 1.48 million registered voters.

In the most telling way imaginable, then, the people of Hong Kong expressed their clear preference for the defenders of democracy. Most of them cast their votes for those who had declared their hostility to, or at least strong reservations about, China's Communist regime.

The result? The opposition to Beijing won thirteen of the twenty seats up for democratic vote, to the jubilation of Martin Lee, president of the Democratic Party, and Emily Lau, courageous director of the "Frontier" movement, both of whom were comfortably elected. Both made a point of remarking, with impeccable logic, that if the whole of the Chamber had been elected by universal suffrage, the pro-Beijing faction would be a small minority.

In any case, the people sent a clear message from the ballot booths to the new masters of Hong Kong. It was an unveiled warning to the Chinese leaders against any temptation to drift toward authoritarianism. A way of showing Beijing that little Hong Kong might prove a David to the great Chinese Goliath in the near future.

Besides, many important Chinese leaders are beginning to wonder if the gift might not turn out to be tainted, and if the Thatcher effect might turn out to be a boomerang.

Several regions of China seeking autonomy will wake up to the fact that if the slogan "one country, two systems," can be applied to Hong Kong, it can be applied to them as well. In Xinjiang, for example, in the northwest of the country, Muslim Uïgurs struggling against the Chinese presence will naturally be tempted to wonder: "Why not us?" There are other examples. Hong Kong is bound to be emulated.

Conclusion: For better or worse, Hong Kong, by taking in Red China, will be an innovator once again.

For the better? The winds of freedom are blowing over Hong Kong, as the poet says. Suppose the winds blow north, toward the People's Republic?

Beijing is going to do everything to "preserve" itself from this insidious southern island. The Chinese regime will try to keep the former British colony in a vacuum, striving, by any means possible, to avoid communications, conversations, and especially comparisons. No doubt about that. But the Communist Chinese may well have gotten more than they bargained for.

For the worse? . . . Vice knows no borders. Within a few weeks of the handover, wagonloads of prostitutes from southern China, mostly young, out-of-work girls, came to taste the delights of Suzy

Wong's paradise. The rejects of socialist planning are starting to come ashore in Hong Kong, ready to try their luck on an island where unemployment is still ridiculously low, despite the economic crisis. The triads use the island as a springboard. In once-safe Hong Kong armed assaults take place in broad daylight, businessmen are mugged. In short, without any drama or turmoil, the island is gradually becoming . . . China.

In any case, Hong Kong will be a kind of pilotfish, revealing how China evolves—or does not. It will be a test case of the sincerity of Beijing's desire to fit into the Western model. Appearances to the contrary, in China, land of yin and yang, shadow and light, anything is possible. For the moment, as we have seen, the People's Republic of China has not faltered. In Hong Kong, it is business as usual. But for how long?

All the same, there is reason to be optimistic, at least for the next few decades. Hong Kong is doubtlessly only a secondary phenomenon for Beijing. For many Chinese leaders the real issue lies to the northeast—Taiwan, which Beijing has sworn to one day bring into its fold.

If the People's Republic succeeds in Hong Kong, there will be no longer any justification for Taipei's opposition to the reunification of the "two Chinas."

Finally, more generally, Asia is acting as a policeman. In Tokyo, Bangkok, Manila—wherever there is concern for regional stability and the geopolitical balance—close attention is being paid to Hong Kong, with a clear message sent to the Chinese leaders that they must leave things be, and not upset the well-being of the people.

For Beijing, the stakes are both domestic and regional. China must make a success of the Hong Kong transplant. If not. . . .